A WOMAN'S WORTH?

To Grandma Simmonds

Enjoy reading

Thanks for your knowledge

2018

Ethlyn Simmonds

A WOMAN'S WORTH?

REVELATION REFLECTION RESOLUTION

CHLOE REBEKAH

Edited By: Rachel K Brown
Cover and Interior Design: Chloe Rebekah
This book is a work of fiction. All characters herein described exist only in the author's imagination with no relation to any persons bearing the same name, living or dead, known or unknown to the author. All names, characters, places, and incidents are either used fictitiously or are the product of the author's imagination. Any resemblance to any person or persons, living or dead, is purely coincidental and unintended

Published by Kindle Direct Publishing

DEDICATION

To each woman, young girl who has ever endured pain longer than they needed to, as they didn't know their worth.

To each woman, young girl who feel they are alone right now. I'm telling you YANA (You Are Not Alone)

To my dear Anita who's joined the angels in heaven. This is for you a true Woman of Worth. You endured a lot of pain here on earth, but you are now in everlasting peace.

CONTENTS

FOREWORD: A WOMAN OF WORTH

I have the pleasure of knowing the author for over 30 years.

It has been interesting to observe her evolve from a young unassuming little girl, to a strong, determined and compassionate young woman, who is a mother of 2 boys.

Chloe Rebekah is an extremely creative individual and has the ability to put her creative skills to developing various projects. She has a natural flare in communicating with others regardless of their status in society. In life, I believe there are people who want to be served and those that have a passion and natural gift in serving others, Chloe Rebekah is a 'Servant' not in the derogatory sense, but in a way that she is willing to go out of her way to do good to others, she will go that extra mile and that is admirable.

Through her written life stories within her book, she has highlighted the real traumatic issues that young girls/women are forced to encounter on a daily basis, these include: sexual abuse, rape, abortion, domestic violence, being estranged and isolated from your biological family, financial challenges etc. and the emotions that are so closely attached.

The author, along with many of us that have picked up this book to read, may be able to identify with many of the experiences that have been shared or at the very least know someone that has. It is important to say that even if you have never experienced any of the situations mentioned, I believe most have had a time when they feel their self-worth is 0%, even below that. There may have been times of wondering why was I even born? What is my purpose on this earth? Life is pointless. Continue reading and you will discover you have purpose and what you feel and what you have experienced does NOT define who you are as a person. You are valuable and there is purpose for your life and the fun I guess, is discovering it!

It is good news to know that we do not have to live as a victim, we can rise from the ashes from the parts of our lives that have been set on fire and burnt out by tragedy. We can walk away metaphorically and literally from those that have consistently caused us pain, but when we say we're walking away it's important not to drag them behind us like a shopping trolley with all our emotional items of anger, resentment, revenge, hate, un-forgiveness... This is not an easy task and it is a daily challenge. For me, day by day I would drag my emotional trolley along through life, some days I would empty some of it and just let go of my issues, other days I felt sure it was completely empty and I was flying free and high only to find that I would hit my emotional ground with a massive bump and would have to start again. If you're in that situation that is OK, just keep addressing the issues until they are no longer an issue. Please don't ignore your pain or the source of it as it will become infected and affect who you were created to be.

The uniqueness of the setting of this book in a Women's Conference, encapsulates and transports you to the very Centre of the action of what is happening in the lives of these women, but gives you as the reader time and space to reflect on your own personal story and challenges you; it is a novel and self-help book rolled into one...amazing!

Having said it is a novel, it is by no means fictitious. It is based upon the reality of what has been experienced by women the author has encountered over the years as well as some of her own.

The overwhelming message that comes through is that although you may have been thrown in a pit, been abused in different ways, you've been abandoned, and you feel you're invisible and forgotten – there is hope.

We can move on from the daily mental torture of our past and present, we don't have to live as an emotional wreck. We don't need to live up to the negative labels that others have attached to us. You're not crazy. The world wouldn't be better off without you.

The truth of the matter is, people that consistently cause pain and distress to others are often suffering in some way themselves from unresolved hurt. This by no means excuses violent, abusive, manipulative and undermining behaviour, but it does show us how imperative it is for us to daily walk in a path of healing, forgiveness and peace, so that we are self-aware and are sensitive to the feelings of others.

If there is some magic solution to ending all pain, please email me and let me know because I want it!! As far as I know there is no potion or lotion that will instantly 'cure' our pain. Allow your pain to work in your favour, over time you will heal, the intensity of the pain will lessen, as we learn to walk from it and help others find their peace.

Know that your Creator loves you and designed you for a special purpose. Surround yourself with people who love and accept you for you and be confident that you are A Woman of Worth.

RACHEL KETURAH

PREFACE

To Every Young Woman,

I've come to a milestone in my life, which I didn't know I'd reached. I've been through so many experiences I can't begin to count. When you reach certain milestones, you feel like it's a rush against time to get everything you dreamed of done. The fairy-tale lifestyle when you're young is that you'll have your ideal career, marriage, family, dream house, dream car. Well, not all will be everyone's desires but, one or two will. The fact is that it's not as easy as 1, 2, 3; they don't always happen in a particular order and how you planned it.

From a young age, I'd always enjoyed reading and writing so it wasn't a surprise at a later age I wanted to write a book. My first attempted approach was to do it on my life so far, but as I wrote, I could feel how easily my fingers would run along the keyboard about happy events but when it came to the point of writing about not so happy ones, my pace would slow down then stop. The problem was, I was unable to relive the times that had passed or bring myself to relay my emotions about them, as the pain was evidently still there. I had uncontrollable tears stream down my face, at the thought of being at that point of my life again as I wrote.

I obviously wasn't ready yet and still needed to heal. So, with this realisation I decided on coming up with a fiction concept, which could show some elements of my life that I could manipulate, in a way that could show the extent of what could happen and still be able to have the same desired outcome.

A Women's Worth is about four women who grow up unaware of each other, until circumstances allows them to cross each other's path. What is be-known to them is that they share the same DNA. The main characters named: Cynthia, Caroline, Celine and Coleen, share with you their journeys from a young age through to a grown woman.

The various sensitive subjects in this book that women go through and not limited to are; domestic violence, drug abuse, child abuse, mental health illnesses, homelessness, imprisonment, rape, abortions and teenage pregnancy. I've had the unfortunate first-hand account of some and know that at the time if I didn't have the right support network, things could have turned out a lot different for me. The others, I have a second-hand account and if I wasn't there for them it could have also been detrimental. I chose these topics as I feel passionate about the effects that it can have on a person and their loved ones, as well as wanting to break the stereotypes and stigmas to allow people to start talking rather than being ashamed.

I've brought two boys into the world that I'm proud of and have been well trained through different careers but it's not how I planned it to be. When I've done tasks, I've wondered how I can use my skills to help someone even if it doesn't benefit me. The joy of writing this book will bring a joint satisfaction of these. I can give every young woman who was once me, growing fast and unaware of the potential challenges she would face, a priceless gift, knowledge. The knowledge of the potential mistakes that can be made, how they can be prevented or how they can be solved. I feel that I have a responsibility to every young woman I meet.

I've met quite a few young women in the various aspects of work I have conducted, and, in those times, I have felt inflicted with sadness, anger and helplessness with some of the stories I've been told, of the treatment some have had to endure. The main issue deeply ridden into these stories was the woman's lack of self-worth, a woman not knowing her self-worth, not loving who she was, not knowing that she is a queen and she should be respected. Life is a very precious gift, although many are unable to have long lives, for me being able to have the opportunity is a blessing. I want to instil, that the world is beautiful, when you take in the good parts and travel and experience what it has to offer.

When you're at the teenage stage of life starting to know yourself, you think you know it all and what you want to do, but I'm here to tell you that you'll have an idea, but it won't be fixed. You can achieve all you want if you put your mind to it but be aware that you can encounter setbacks in your timing and choices may need to be altered in a way depending on your circumstances at the time. Overall, enjoy the journey; learn along the way, even when your body may be changing as well as your emotions and your hormones, which may affect the way you react to certain situations.

It won't be easy, but it'll be okay with the right people around you, the right frame of mind, the strength within and the knowledge, you'll be able to strive through. The world is a scary place I'm not going to sugar-coat it. There are liars, murderers, deceivers and people who say they wish you well but really want to see you fail. Be able to know the difference of those you can trust to those you can't. If you know something is wrong, do right. Our decisions have consequences, some less likely to wither away than others.

For example, I wanted to show different angles of abuse as a child and an adult to show how easy it is to develop a mental illness from the trauma you've suffered, if not dealt with earlier on in life it can have a detrimental effect later on in life. I believe you shouldn't be ashamed to ask for help or to share with others. I've not had the great portfolio of healthy male relationships and that's what partly sparked my motivation to keep pushing my spurts, in addition to being part of the research process along with a variety of blogs. I sometimes had an idea, but didn't know how I could make a connection, or for it be realistic. I realised throughout writing that realistic can appear unrealistic in reality, as what you may think is unbelievable is in fact someone's life.

I've evaluated my life so far and produced some commandments I'd have wanted to be told to help me along my way through my teenage to adult years. Here's my gift to you, I hope they are of great assistance.

25 Commandments For You

1.   **Put you first** – Do what makes you happy before deciding on what will make someone else happy. Your happiness comes first and foremost.

2.   **Know yourself** – Who are you? What are your values? What do you believe in? Do not dismiss and change the qualities that make you. You are unique, special and should not change for anyone. Remember you cannot change anyone but yourself.

3.   **Do not put off what you can do today for tomorrow** – Yes, you may have tomorrow, but some things are better taken care of when the intent for action is there. You don't know what may arise tomorrow for putting off a particular task and then you end up with a consequence that could have been avoided.

4.   **Be wary of who you trust** – Not everyone will be a friend or who they say they are. Some people will come into your life in disguise as someone wanting the best for you, but it may not be real. Find out their intentions sooner rather than later. If you have a feeling that something doesn't feel right, go with it, you'll most likely be right.

5.   **Keep positive** – Sometimes that is all you can hold onto to keep pushing forward. It can get so hard that you can't even hold onto a person's word, but you have to believe in yourself that it can only get better. Take it a minute at a time.

6.   **Take in everything as experiences and learn from them** – Everything did not just happen by chance. There is a ripple effect of everything that each and every one of us do which triggers an event. We are here to experience and take in life, our surroundings, accept our choices and live with them. If you do not want to repeat an experience, don't repeat choosing the same choice, learn and have a new outcome.

7.   **Love does not hurt** – Love is patient, love is kind. It does not envy, it does not boast, it is not proud. It does not dishonour others, it is not self-seeking, it is not easily angered, it keeps no record of wrongs. Love does not delight in evil but rejoices with the truth. It always protects, always trusts, always hopes, always perseveres. Love never fails. 1 Corinthians chapter 13 verses 4-8.

8.   **Be patient** – Wanting is not the same as needing. You need oxygen, you need water, you do not need the latest gadget. If it was meant for you it will come to you, when you least expect it. Live within your means. Be patient with the things you want, that are life changing. A pet is not just for Christmas, a baby will in time grow up and won't just be a cute face but need love, care and attention.

9.   **Plan and use each moment wisely** – Time is not owed to us, it can come and go in a blink of an eye with no warning. The time you're given, use it wisely. Do not waste it on things that will not help you grow and take you to where you want to be.

10.   **Surround yourself with positive people** – You'll be surprised how much negativity can consume you, drain your energy. Remove yourself away from those people who can only speak and openly have negative attitudes. You cannot progress with these types of people, they are energy stealers.

11.   **Love yourself first** – How can you expect someone to love you if you don't know what loving yourself is like? You need to love your own company, love your image, love your personality. On a whole, be able to love yourself as exactly who you are. When a love type of relationship comes your way, it will be more of a bonus and if it happens to go away, you can go back to your own company. Real love does not need to be in a partnership of a sexual kind, to feel what love is can be as great as spending quality time with friends and family. It's not to say we don't want it or need it but in all reality we all may not get it.

12.   **Do not take out finance on a possession unless it holds value** – You want to be able to make a profit not make a deficit. When it comes to purchasing think about what you are going to gain, what will hold its value in years to come.

13.   **Learn, learn, learn** – Knowledge is power. It can be a powerful weapon to getting and knowing the truth. When you know the truth, no one can fool you or tell you different. So, read, study, research, record, analyse.

14.   **You have more to offer than a pretty face and what's in between your legs. You have a bright future ahead of you** – Anyone can give you a compliment and there will always be temptation and lust. Once something is done it cannot be undone. If someone respects you for who you are, you will not have to offer up your dignity.

15.   **Anyone can tell you nice words and promise you the world, you need to see actions for what they are** – Are they genuine and what are their intentions?

16.   **Believe that you can do anything without the need of a partner or someone to support you, you are stronger than you think** - It doesn't mean you can't accept help but be fearless. We focus so much on the fear itself that we don't stop to think about what could be on the other side of fear. Compare fear and faith in terms of what we don't see but believe is there. One will stop you the other will keep you going. When there are tasks you feel scared to do, do it with fear. Believe you can...

17.   **Some people like the idea of you but can't accept the reality of you** – The way you carry yourself, people are in awe of you. They want a piece of you, but because you are strong minded and know what your future holds, they can feel inferior if they are unsure of their journey or do not want to make the effort to progress.

18.   Have a role model – If you have no one around you to inspire you, look for someone elsewhere who you can look up to, talk to, mentor you and genuinely wants the best for you.

19. **Forgive** – You don't want to, but it's the only way to stop the hurt. People hurt you not realising that they have or the extent, accept it. Whilst you have all the anger, hurt and oppression the other person is getting on with their life. Transfer all of those feelings positively and if it is to be, that person will get their just dessert elsewhere, it is not for you to dish it. It's said, that when you can't remember why you're hurt, that's when you're healed.

20. **Good friends you don't find** – They come to you, they've been there, stayed and never gone away. They accept you for who you are, they do not want to see you hurt and they want the best for you.

21. **You don't need to say yes** – If you want to say no, say no. Do not feel under pressure for doing what you want.

22. **Honesty** – is the best policy, in everything. Don't say it's only a little white lie. A lie is a lie, no matter how big or small. I'd rather cry to the truth than laugh at a lie, keep that in mind when you don't want someone lying to you.

23. **Loyalty** – This right here keep in high regard. The loyalty of others keep them near, your loyalty in return will keep others near.

24. **Be a fighter** – Fight for what you believe in, fight for what you want and don't stop until you do. This is if it's not untoward and is meant for you.

25. **Be YOU** – Be that person you want to be proud of, the you that inspires others, the you that promotes positive change, the you that will achieve to be all she wants to.

As you've come to the end, it's time to begin. Enjoy reading as much as I've enjoyed writing.

I AM MY SISTERS KEEPER

Where was Eve's sister in the garden of Eden?

Was that the reason Eve traded her dignity for disgrace for Adam? Is Eve the reason all women bear pain in childbirth? Genesis 3:16.

My sister's, my queen's, I need to know can you hear me? I need you to listen, take heed to the words that I speak. As I am... My sister's keeper, I have a responsibility to you my sister... to break it down... to you, so you no longer have to feel suffocated, with your emotions that are giving uncertainty to the problem which is evidently there. Our bond is made by passion with purpose. Together we are strong, together we are a rock that cannot be broken.

I am angry, can you agree? The man has left you belittled, mentally, emotionally maybe even physically; invisible/visible scars of the manipulation, disfiguration, persuasion, invasion succumbed from rejection and deception. You are the backbone, the rib of a man. You sister complete the man, you are strong, special, a nurturer, believer of I am with a positive close. If I tell you... You are!

Do you feel at times like you're not worthy, like you need to metamorphic into this being that likely doesn't exist, to make this human form with different genitalia feel secure with oneself?

I'm tired, I'm tired as much as you of living a Jekyll and Hyde lifestyle, I just, want to be me.

The me that the media would otherwise like to portray, of imperfections being less than beauty. A photo taken and posted giving the option to filter out those flaws, which should be showing the realness of the true image, and that is what it truly signifies at that time.

Picture this: A career-driven woman with bags under her eyes, after having a long week at work to seal her promotion. Hashtag drivenwoman, hashtag bagsundereyes, hashtag idontcare, hashtag igotmyselfpromoted, hashtag womangoals. A woman's worth is more than the colour of her skin, the amount of money she makes, if she has kids or none. It is her knowing as a woman, what is her value? What does she deserve? What will she not stand for? What does she need, to fundamentally do, to regularly sustain her belief that she is worth more than...? And be destined for the purpose of her intentions.

My conditioned mind leads me to believe I don't need a man and can fend for itself as I've had no example of... a real man. The absent father that leaves his daughter in a vicious circle of unresolved issues of trust, disorders, abandonment, conclusive root instituting her promiscuity, premarital births, poor choices. The abusive man leaving their partner guilty, blamed and shamed. The womaniser who draws in, to dash away any sex on legs as that is what he sees, resulting in a woman feeling bitter, scorned and even insecure in her body.

Whatever kind of man it'll be white, black, Asian, thin, fat. If he is trying to bring YOU down as a woman, he is not a man. A man knows a real woman, and what a woman is worth. A real man will appreciate, respect, value, guide, motivate and stimulate you, in more ways than one. You won't have to change your personality or appearance but be the better version of yourself striving together as Kings and Queens of your thrones.

I, Cynthia, say thank you in the mic, and call up the rest of our team; Caroline, Coleen, and Kayla to the podium. This will be our first A.W.W (A Womans Worth) Convention, where we will be conducting a variety of talks, workshops and presentations, to celebrate the victories of women who have fought their battles and are on the next step of their journey to healing.

The organisation first got established after Coleen had finished studying Psychology. She purchased a building and transformed it into a Centre from capital left for her in her mother's will. Her dream was to be able to have an environment where women in dire restraint could feel comfortable to share their experiences. A place to let go of their fears, troubles that they had. Her mind at the time she said, thought but, "What does Yana mean?" "What does it stand for?" She explained, she started to research what it meant, and the results she found was "God answers". Then as she gave deeper thought about what each letter stood for, she came up with: You Are Not Alone. It was to her realisation that there were many women around her, in the local area, the country, the world that were experiencing similar matters she had, but were unaware that someone else could actually be there to support and encourage them so they aren't alone or suffer in silence.

We've maintained a structure to ensure each woman who attends the Centre and is part of the movement, embrace what it conveys in terms of what is positive about being a woman, positive about the future, positive outcomes of struggles.

We then discovered via internet research what the image of having the name Yana looked like, and that it would be given to a very gorgeous sweet girl. The representation of her being very kind and very beautiful and not like anyone else you would ever meet. She would always put other's needs ahead of her own and the power to insistently make everything better.

She would be always positive and have the ability to put a smile on anybody's face. For a Yana the sky would not be the limit, there would be no limit at all for a Yana. She would like to make dreams and push herself until she made those dreams a reality.

A Yana would be the type of girl that you would look at for the first time and know that she is probably "The One". She would be an amazing cook and be great around children. She would make a great mum and wife one day.

If you ever were to meet a Yana in your life, she would be the one for sure you could never let go, because a woman like her only comes around once in a lifetime. To be able to come across this information was an affirmation, perfect. This would be the representation Coleen explained she would want young women to admire and inspire to be, if they were lost and trying to find themselves.

Now so we can begin, myself, Caroline, Coleen and Kayla will be conducting presentations together on, destruction leads to empowerment and establishing the ultimate purpose of A Woman's Worth. If you look inside your individual packs, you will find out where your designated session will be first. In Hall 1 will be Kayla and Caroline and Hall 2 Coleen and me.

Hi ladies I'm Caroline, welcome to the first of many, hopefully of A.W.W Conventions. I feel that, so we all can be open with each other today and build confidence together, I need to share my story. I am going to start by reading the last letter written from Kayla's late mother Celine who committed suicide in prison. Here goes:

This will most likely be the last time you hear of me as I no longer can take being confined in this cell. I have experienced a rollercoaster of emotions; hate, guilt, fear and pain, stemming from life before I got in here. I don't believe I should entirely have been sentenced to imprisonment, as I was only trying to protect a friend who was getting hurt. It was an accident; I didn't mean to kill him.

All my life I have metaphorically seen men get away with murder, compared to the ladies who I'm in here with. They aren't real criminals, most of them have committed non-violent crimes, I'm one of the 16 percent who actually has, and even so my act wasn't premeditated. I would say that half of them in here have either suffered from domestic violence, emotional, physical and sexual abuse in childhood, such as myself and what they're really needing is therapy treatment for the abuse. When I wake up each day, it is a routine of; wake up, eat, work, eat, sleep, repeat. I can understand how inmates will develop OCD trying to control any little thing in this environment, along with anxiety, depression or psychosis but I refuse for that to be me.

We have no privacy when going to the toilet; as you know, it is in the cell with us. When we need to do a number two, we signal our other room-mates by burning an incense stick beforehand and flush immediately to try not to offend, by allowing the smell to fester in the air for too long.

There is constant banging, noises of all kinds of inmates screaming, groaning, moaning and crying. The worst is when a prisoner's visitor hasn't turned up; then, you really hear an inmate kick off, as she tries to fight off the guards whilst being taken back to her cell, kicking and screaming.

It's difficult to know who to trust in here, you have to be mindful of each action you make as any action of friendliness may convey that you want sex with them.

Out of everything I have to endure in here, not seeing my kids is the ultimate heartbreaker. This is the first time I have ever let them both out my sight, and now they're both momentarily staying in two different foster homes either end of the country, it is near impossible for me to see them. I miss them so much. As I calculate how long I'll be in here, with each day passing by, not knowing a precise date when I can or will ever see them again.

I see it if I take my life now, rather than later I will remove the emptiness and heartbreak in an instant. I've had suicidal thoughts before I got here but the kids gave me purpose not to, now I'm certain there's no way out of my situation and it will not change any time soon. I'll not be coming out for a while and in that time, who knows what my mental state will be and if I'll even be able to care for them both again.

When I found out I was pregnant with my first child and daughter, Kayla. I made a promise that I would not give her the life I did. I did all I could to prepare myself to be a teenage mother, as I wanted to make sure this would be the beginning of a new start for me. The prophecy I'd been told of not amounting to anything, being worthless, would become void, as I would be bringing her into this world and she'd give me the purpose to become the best part of me. As I used to lay in the bath and rub my stomach, being able to see her grow bigger each day, I spoke to her and told her all the dreams I had, and be able to fulfil, with her there by my side, proud. Proud to say, "That's my mum."

I dreamt before meeting her face, how she'd look, what I'd get her to wear, the baby smell you can't get rid of as it transfers onto your clothes. She'd bring a contagious feeling of happiness to everyone that would meet her.

The thing is I broke my promise to her, I let her down. I wasn't there when she needed me the most, plaiting her hair for school, the bedtime stories all seem pointless times we spent together, as I wasn't there when she needed me the most. It's sad she felt she couldn't come to me for help, as the person hurting her, that she thought loved her just like me, didn't. Events happened so quickly that I was unable to talk to her about how she was feeling, how she was coping. I am sure she will remain strong as I did suffering in silence, as I am part of her. I'm probably not going to see her graduate from primary school and move up to be a teenager in secondary and it breaks me that I'll miss everything.

I just need her to know that I always loved her and her brother Paul Jnr. and nothing was ever their fault. One day I hope they'll be able to understand why I did what I did, by knowing what I've been through.

DADDY

"You going to let daddy make it better?"

"Does that feel nice?"

"Daddy just wants his little princess to be happy."

"I'll have to take you shopping to get you some new panties, these seem to have a hole in them."

"That'll be nice, won't it?"

"You going to make daddy happy now?"

Huuuuu-h... I wake up in my usual state after the same reoccurring nightmare. Sweat dripping off my forehead, bed feeling soaked like I'd been lying in my own piss. This had been happening since I was five.

I couldn't seem to get rid of the images, the touch, the smell, out of my psyche, haunting me even now, I'm twenty-five years old, grown with my own children.

I assume you're wondering; did I tell someone? I did. I told the one person I thought would listen; tell me it would be okay, that he won't be able to hurt me anymore. Yes, I'm talking about my mother. Well the so-called woman who gave birth to me and became privileged with the title, though was never entitled.

She knew deep down, I'm sure of it. Why he always took longer in my room at bedtime, when she went to work, anytime I was left alone with him. I guess she didn't want to jeopardise her relationship, as he had been there for us when my so-called birth father deserted us.

Why? Why would she repeatedly allow him to hurt me like that? Choose a man over her child, she carried, gave birth to. I couldn't tell you, but I'd spit on her grave, that's what I'd do if something was to happen to this pathetic, pitiful, insignificant being.

I started going to the priest for confessions from as far back as I remember, to confess the things I was doing to my stepfather, so it'd deter him to stop. They were minor little things, like milk of magnesia in his tea, cleaning the toilet with his toothbrush, drawing pins in his shoes. The priest told me it wasn't healthy to revenge and that I needed to use another avenue to release this type of negative energy. In a hope that his advice would work, I conjured up the courage and told my mother, and she didn't believe me. What was I to do now? I returned back to the priest, he said, "Jesus says to forgive seventy-seven times seven. You need to forgive your mother, for she knows not what she's done, and move forward with your life if you can't face reporting it to the police." If my mother couldn't believe me, why would the police? I didn't forgive her, but I moved on.

"Celine, are you going to get these kids breakfast, I need to get ready for work?"

"Yes, I'm coming Paul," I responded back, trying to make sure it projected down the hallway, as I was in the bedroom and the door was shut.

Paul was my kids' dad. We had moved in together after I got a property with the council when the pitiful being kicked me out at five months pregnant. Honestly, I can't even say if my daughter (five) is Paul's or my stepfather's. So much was going on at the time, there was no head space for anything. Paul and I were happy, and he said he'd stick around, so I thought there was no point in rocking the boat.

I walk to the living room, "Morning my little cherubs," kissing them both on the forehead. My daughter is Kayla, a spitting image of me, small eyes, chubby cheeks, tight curled hair and deep dark clear skin. My son Paul Jnr is not too far off eighteen months, a spitting image of his dad.

"So, what do you want mummy to get you both for breakfast?"

I hear the front door shut, Paul's gone to work with no say again. We're not talking, he's sleeping on the settee at the moment, as I just found out I'm eight weeks pregnant. Great, that's all I need right now.

I met Paul just after I left school, he used to hang out with the local guys around my area at the shops. As I ventured to the shops to get milk or buy another essential, our eyes would connect, and he'd say 'hi' and I'd smile.

He had a beautiful smile that gave me goosebumps, the first guy I actually fancied. This would happen a lot, us crossing paths and having minimal chit chat until one day he asked for my number. I gave it to him and we started talking on the phone, which eventually led to my friends and me hanging out with him and his friends at the shops. I felt happy that I was able to have some kind of normal teenage life instead of what I had to endure at home.

The first time I invited him to my house I had a free house, and as we sat on the bottom of my bed laughing, we looked at each other and he leant over and kissed me. He told me he loved me and even though I knew he couldn't have, I believed him, and we ended up sleeping together. It became more regular and things seemed to be progressing seriously, so I built up the courage to invite him round to introduce him to my mother as my boyfriend. She was happy for me, but my stepfather wasn't, this angered him.

I could tell as he'd look at Paul in a certain 'offish' way then Paul had to ask me, "What is his problem with me?" I'd say to him, "Nothing, he's just being protective of me I guess," but the fact was it was jealousy. I knew this, as when my stepfather got the opportunity, he'd argue with me and call me names, saying, "You do know he only wants you for sex not like me," and then he'd grab me and rape me there and then. It came to the point I would show no feeling and lie motionless as he would hold me down. There was no getting away from him, living in the same house. It was apparent that it affected mine and Paul's relationship in the bedroom department as I was uninterested. I had to reassure him that there was no one I wanted more than him, as he thought I was cheating on him.

When we ended up moving in together, things were better as we started to make plans for us to have Kayla, but things started to get sour after she was born. I took it as we were under a lot of strain with having another body to look after, with getting to know each other whilst living under the same roof. Overall mine and Paul's relationship isn't the best, but I know he loves me. When the house isn't in order when he comes home from work, or he's had a bad day at work, he takes it out on me, but I brush it off as it could be worse. I guess I need to be more understanding of his needs at times, as he's only working hard for our future. If I know he's going to react badly to a situation, I should do what is expected of me shouldn't I?

"Okay kids let's try our best to be early today, mummy has got a busy day ahead," placing each of their breakfast bowls in front of them.

The kids start to eat their breakfast as I get myself ready and pack all of our bags ready for University, nursery and school. I should be more organised from the night before I know, but as I'd got in late from work at the bar, I was so knackered, I crawled straight into bed.

Currently I'm having to juggle my architecture course at University, I'm in my second year and I've got a part time job at a bar which I do three times a week. I need to make ends meet, to maintain my home and provide for the kids. I don't see much of Paul's wage. He buys the food shopping and the rest goes in savings, and the one thing he says he needs to make sure he can buy for himself, is his weed. The weed is like a gift to himself after finishing work to help him unwind.

I've given Paul Jnr. a wipe down and put his clothes on ready to go in his pram, so I call out to Kayla, "Are you ready?"

She doesn't reply so I go to her room.

"Kayla," as I open her bedroom door.

"Yes mummy," she says.

"Couldn't you hear me calling you?"

"No mummy," as she crouches by her bed.

"What's the matter, sweetie?"

"I wet my bed, sorry mummy."

"Don't worry about it, these things happen sometimes."

"Get your bag and coat and stand by the door with your brother while I get your bed covers and protector and put them in the washing machine.

After I tear off the covers, I open up the window to get some air into the room.

"Okay we all ready? Let's go," I say to them both.

We make our way out of the house, towards the nursery and school. They are close in proximity to each other and near our home, so we walk, plus the fresh air and exercise does us good. We drop Paul Jnr. first, then Kayla so we can have some mummy daughter time on the way to school and in the playground before the bell rings. I enjoy the little time we have together, we talk about what she likes doing at school, what she wants to be when she's older, what places she likes to visit. She's very fond of the Bratz character dolls. I feel they're for older girls because of their fashion sense but I guess it's no harm as they're only dolls. We get to the school and Kayla sees her friends, so they play hopscotch and skipping ropes. I watch as she plays, I can't believe how she is growing up so quickly. The bell rings so Kayla runs and gives me a kiss before she heads towards the school door entrance, making sure she turns back and waves goodbye.

I leave the school and head to the train station, three stops on the tram and one train out the city for forty minutes to get to the University.

We were learning about nineteenth-century architecture today, identifying different architectural styles and seeing how they were revived into Neo architecture.

As I was in my second year, I had the chance to study abroad but with the kids it wouldn't have been feasible. I was not resentful towards the kids for being unable to travel, as I was still moving forward in doing something positive for their future and there would be plenty of time to go abroad as a family.

It became closer to the end of the day around 2pm and Kayla's class teacher rang and asked if it would be possible to come in to talk to her tomorrow, as she knew Kayla would be in after-school club today, so I'd be picking her up later from there. She said it wasn't anything serious, but she just wanted to make me aware of something.

Although she said it was nothing to worry about, I couldn't do anything but worry. Kayla was a bright girl; she loved school and did what was asked of her.

I decided to catch the train back nevertheless, so I left University early to make it back to the school in time of it finishing.

I got to the school on time and saw Kayla's teacher outside waiting at the classroom door, letting kids out as they spotted their parents. I started to approach the door, once I saw nearly all the children go; before I could say anything, Kayla's class teacher said, "I wasn't expecting you, but I'm happy you came."

"It sounded important so there was no hesitation," I said.

"Do you mind if I just grab another teacher to sit in with us, it's just procedure."

"Yeah that's fine."

"Okay, come into the classroom."

She offered me a seat and we all sat down at the children's desks, arranged in a way so that we could all face each other.

"So today we had P.E and at first Kayla was refusing to get changed. She said she didn't want to do P.E today. I asked her why? She said she was tired, and her legs were hurting."

"Okay, I'm listening," I said.

"Well she eventually came around to take part and started to get changed, but she was trying to hide herself, getting changed in the corner of the room. I left her to it as she was cooperating with me and when she had her kit on, she followed her fellow classmates to the hall. Whilst in the hall I asked them all to sit with their legs crossed on the floor. As I am explaining what we'd be doing today - standing in front of the class. I spot Kayla with her hands down her shorts rubbing her private parts. I felt concerned with what she was doing, but so as not to bring too much attention to it with the rest of the class, I said Kayla let's put our hands on our lap and keep still."

"This doesn't sound like usual behaviour of Kayla not wanting to do P.E; I'll speak to her when we get home thanks."

"How has Kayla been at home?" her teacher asks.

"She's been fine, she has her moments being disobedient but that's children for you," I reply.

"Okay, have you had any new friends and family around her lately?"

"No, it's just me, her dad and brother. Why? What are you getting at? What's with all the questions?"

"Just trying to get the full picture of how Kayla is at home, as her behaviour seems to be changing and we want to make sure that we, the school are doing the best to accommodate her if she needs any extra support in any way."

"Well, if that's all it is... Don't want any insinuations made, I'm a good mother."

"We're not disputing that, we know you have maintained a genuine interest in your child since she has started this school and she is one of the brightest kids in the class."

"Will that be all?"

"If you haven't got any further questions."

"No not at the moment. Please can you do your best to keep me informed of any other incidents though?"

"Of course,"

"Okay thanks," I awkwardly mumble as I shake their hand and walk out the door to go to the after-school club hut to pick up Kayla.

They release Kayla for me and we start to walk out of the school towards the nursery. I feel that now is probably the best time to try and talk to her as there'll be distractions when we get home.

"How was school today?"

"It was ok mummy."

"What did you do today at school?"

"I did adding, takeaway and literacy."

"What about P.E?"

"I did P.E too."

"Miss Laney said that you didn't want to do P.E today, is that right?"

Kayla shakes her head looking down.

"Is there any reason you didn't want to?"

"I...I... just didn't want to and my legs were hurting me."

"Okay, so there's nothing upsetting you that you want to tell mummy?"

"No mummy... You're not going to tell daddy, are you?"

"If you don't want me to... You did P.E in the end didn't you?"

"Yes, mummy I did"

"Okay then. If you ever want to talk to me, I'm here"

"Okay mummy."

"Good, let's get your brother then and we can make some dinner together when we get in."

We have a peaceful evening, me and the kids, making the dinner whilst playing music and having a laugh. It was such a different atmosphere when it was just the three of us, I liked it. When I put the kids to bed, I waited for Paul to get in.

BOO HOO HOO

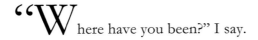"here have you been?" I say.

"You're not my keeper" Paul snaps back.

"I was worried, I've been calling you and it's been going to answerphone."

"Don't you worry."

"Why you got to be like that?"

"I'm not arguing with you, leave me be."

"Okay cool...."

"You go to the clinic today?" Paul asks.

".... Yeah"

"You get it done?"

"No, they wouldn't allow me to go through with it, as I was upset."

"What you mean?"

"Exactly how I said. They wouldn't do the procedure unless they felt certain I wanted to get it done."

"You're going back there tomorrow, and you better hold back the tears!"

"I can't... I don't want to," I'm whimpering at this point. My heart was breaking right now, at the thought I'd have to kill my baby.

"Well you have to; I'm not ready to have another child. It's not like I was even down for a second child."

"It's my body, not yours... you just don't care."

"No, I don't.... Grrr, you get me so angry. Why can't you just do what you're told?"

"I can't go through with it again, that's why..."

"Do what you want then, but don't think I'll have anything to do with it, if you do!"

"You're so horrible."

I pick up the closest object to me and throw it.

"What the f@%! you doing? You want to start breaking shit now... Yeah... yeah? Shall I join in and be a child throwing its toys out of the pram?"

He starts getting photo frames of us and drops them on the floor breaking them.

"STOP IT!!! STOP IT!!!" I shout.

I start walking towards him to try get him to stop.

"D'you think you're Jesus walking on water? There's f@%£*?! glass on the floor you stupid bitch!"

"I hate you!" grabbing his wrists shaking him, whilst he tries to restrain me to stop.

"I hate you too!!!! Believe me!" he says.

I'm standing there crying, unsure of what to do with myself.

"Boo hoo hoo... Look at you. You're a mess. You're not fit to be a mother." As he pushes me down to the floor, he tells me, "Whilst you're down there, you might as well clean this shit up."

I'm lying there, tears streaming down my face, nose drooling with snot. As Paul walks past me, he kicks me in my stomach and mumbles,

"Maybe you'll do something about it now; you couldn't cope with bearing a disabled child could you?"

He kisses his teeth with a mutter under his breath of, "You make me sick," and slams the front door, leaving me helpless on the floor.

The morning comes, and Paul hasn't come back home.

Kayla comes in and says, "Mummy, are you and daddy going to break up?"

"What would make you say that darling?"

"I could hear you and daddy shouting at each other last night. Is it because of me?"

"No, no, not at all, don't ever think that, okay? It could never be your fault."

She starts crying, I cuddle her apologetically. "I'm so sorry I wish you didn't have to hear us. I'll try my best to make sure that it doesn't happen again."

I didn't like how we were putting our daughter through this, it wasn't fair. She was so young she shouldn't have had to deal with all of this.

I tell her to go in her room and put her favourite DVD on, so she can take her mind off everything. As she heads to her room, I go onto our computer in the living room to accumulate some research for Uni I go to click on the internet browser but it's already open and there are tabs open, which Paul must have forgotten to close.

I wouldn't usually pry but something told me to click on them, and to my surprise there are a few items that revealed a lot. The one tab showed his Facebook messenger conversations with a girl called Amina. I read on, and he's been seeing her. They talk about when they are next going to meet, how he'll be unable to meet up with her tonight, as he's looking after Kayla whilst I'm at work, how we're not together but he's still here for the kids.

The liar! It continues to say he'll be over tomorrow, which gets me thinking that he should be at work at the time he's saying. I then click to go onto online banking as something doesn't seem right. I get into our account and it shows he hasn't been paid for a couple of months; I'm thinking what is going on? I check on the savings account it's, empty. Is this guy taking the piss? I'm here breaking my back. I assume he's lost his job, but he's definately cheating and I'm looking after our kids, working and studying on top of everything else.

I hear the front door, I'm instantly seeing red and want answers from him. He comes into the living room and I'm

staring at him.

"What are you looking at?" he demands.

"What you playing at?" I respond.

He comes over and sees that I've been snooping.

"What the f@%! you doing looking at my shit?" he shouts.

"How could you?

"Do what?"

"Lie to me, cheat on me."

"Don't know what you're on about," his tone of voice lowers.

"It's all there Paul," pointing at the screen.

"Whatever, I haven't got time for this shit."

"I'm not having it, you've got to go."

He laughs, "I'm not going anywhere."

"Yes, you are," I scream. "I'm not taking all this anymore."

"Well unless you can physically remove me out of this flat, I'm not going anywhere."

I try to push him out of the living room door but he's hardly budging and he's pushing me back with force, gripping onto my arm.

"Just go," I'm saying repeatedly.

"No!"

"Leave me alone and let me be." I cry.

"No!" he says defiantly.

I give up the struggle, leave the room heading to my bedroom, shut the door and sit behind it crouching with my head in my knees crying. I want it to stop, I'm not happy, I want it all to end, it's a rhetorical cycle over and over again. Always the same chapter, same verse, just a new day, different cause. He begins banging the door with his fist, "Let me in!"

"Go away," I shout back.

"No... You want to ruin my life, I'll ruin yours," he shouts back.

I cry louder.

"No one's coming to your rescue, no-one cares not even your mother," he laughs.

He continues to attack me, "Boo hoo hoo, is that all you can do? I'm Celine and I'm so hard done by. Boo hoo hoo... Change the record," as he continues to bang the door.

I move away from the door, get into bed and cover myself with the duvet so he can't see my face and I'm not having to hear him say anything else. I sense him coming towards the duvet, trying to uncover me, "Leave me alone."

"I'm sorry, okay. You just make me angry. Come on let's talk," he says trying, to act more calmly.

"I want you to go away Paul, all you do is hurt me."

"You know what they say, you only hurt the ones you love."

"Not like this. You torment me repeatedly until I feel helpless. I don't want to feel like this anymore."

He tries to hold me and bring my head towards his chest to comfort me, stroking my hair at the same time.

"We'll work it out, we always do, don't we babe? It's just a little setback but we can get back on track. Calm down, get your breath back, I'll get you a cup of tea."

He leaves the room and heads to the kitchen. I hear him on the way down the hallway, open Kayla's door and say, "Everything's okay princess don't worry."

What a prick, I'm saying in my head. He behaves like a psycho towards me and then he tries to function like everything's normal. There's something wrong with him and there's something wrong with me. I feel like I'm not strong enough to follow through with getting rid of him, so I take him back to continue with this heartache. I need help but who can I go to? He's right I don't have anyone, plus he's such a smooth talker, who'd believe me that he treats me this way.

He comes back and gives me the cup of tea, "There you are, this should make you feel better."

He sits there as I sip on the tea. I'm contemplating what should I do. I know I can't have this child now. He's not good for me, and it's not healthy to bring another child into this, but I know I don't want to go through with it either and make him feel like he's won. I feel so lost. In deep deliberation with my thoughts, I sit on the bed alone. I make the decision that I'll call the clinic, to go ahead with an abortion as soon as I get the chance.

HOW CAN I BE OF SERVICE?

A few days past and though Paul was trying to be on his best behaviour, I knew I had to follow through with my decision and go to the clinic today for an abortion.

When I get there, I check in. It's not too busy so I choose to sit anywhere. I'm waiting a while, so I end up reading all the posters on the wall. A young lady walks in the waiting room to join me, she is prestige looking, designer from head to toe, strutting with her Louis Vuitton bag, hung on her shoulder, Dolce shades hiding her beautiful jade eyes (which I later see), emphasising her goldilocks hair. She decides to sit right next to me, though there's a choice of chairs surrounding the room.

"Why you looking so sorry for yourself?" she asks me.

I look at her, "Why'd you think?"

"It's not that bad. Who wants a bratty, crying baby anyway?"

"Well I've got two, of what you call them, and they're neither bratty or crying babies!"

"One minute," she says. Her phone is ringing.

"Hello this is Daphne; how can I be of service to you?... Mum why are you calling this line, you know I can't accept personal calls, this is strictly for business, I hope it's important... Stop yourself there, I've got another call coming through... Hello this is Daphne, how can I be of service to you?... Okay sugar, I can be of assistance. How does 8pm sound to you?... Can I meet you at that new bar just by Claymore Row...? Yeah...Yeah... That's great see you tonight."

Assuming she's taken her mum off hold, she continues, "Okay, so what's so important?.... No, I didn't forget Nanny and Granddad's meal I'll be there. See you later."

Putting the phone down she turns her body to face mine.

"I'm Caroline by the way," putting her hand out to shake mine.

"I thought your name was Daphne?" shaking her hand.

"Okay, let me explain to eliminate any confusion, Daphne is my stage name that I use for my business. Caroline is what you will formerly address me by.

As you can probably sum up I am a woman of poise, hahahahahahaha, couldn't help myself. Who am I kidding? I live in Lore Folks with my mother and my grandparents, they live in another part of the house, don't get to see them very much.

Anyway, I went to an all-girls school, had my own pony, used to ride it on weekends, had elocution lessons (much good it done me), was in this circle that mothers and daughters are in, do afternoon tea and all that shah-bang bla bla bla bla.

I've never done without, had everything, still have everything to be honest. Don't know who my dad is, there's never been a mention of him, couldn't care less, can't miss what you don't have. All I do know is that he's.... let me say it a bit quietly... black!

I know, if you meet my family you'll know they're as racist as they come. They don't even use the word black. Its n****, and you know how black people are when a white person throws that word around hmmmm... huummmm..... Exactly. They're alright with me I guess, as my complexion is veeery fair as you can see, and with my goldilocks hair you can't tell. I haven't got a problem with black people, I'd have a black man any day, they sure like me too. I seem to get asked if I've had my lips done, as I've got them plump kissable lips. You know what I mean? Anyway, I tell them that I haven't but that's as far as the conversation goes. I do wonder sometimes who my dad's side of the family is, if I've ever walked past them, seen them on a night out, but I guess I'll never know as it's not a topic for discussion. She paused for a slight breath, "On a brighter note, my life's great, I make it a little more interesting with the white stuff and then life's first class. Haven't got a special man in my life, other than a few sugar daddies that I see from time to time to take me shopping and I escort them to some great events. I'd say it's a win win, they get a beautiful lady on their arm and I get quite a bit of cash."

I look at her in amazement. "Do you ever stop? You have probably spoke about yourself for the last 10 minutes. Why are you talking to me?" I say.

"Got nothing better to do. You look like you got a pretty face under them blood shot eyes and damp face, best fix yourself up before they have their say," as she tilts her head towards the direction of the clinic staff to make me aware who she was talking about.

"Yes, I'm very aware of what'll happen if I don't," I assure her.

"So, what do you do when you're not being a mother?" Caroline asks me.

"I study, and I've got a part time job."

"Okay, do they pay enough?"

"It gives me just the right amount I need to survive, so yes."

"Well I have regular clients who have friends, that I could book you in with... That's if you ever get a bit strapped for cash, it pays well."

"No thanks."

"Well Miss Snobbery, it can't be that bad, look at my face compared to yours, who looks happier?"

My name gets called so I stand up to be ushered to where I need to go. As I head out, Caroline slips me her business card in my hand saying, "Well if you change your mind call me." She winks at me, whilst I shake my head disapprovingly and walk out putting her card in my bag.

I'm firstly ushered into a room, where they give me an ultrasound scan to ensure I am positively pregnant, and inform me how many weeks I am, they then brief me on which treatment I will require. As I am being examined I am told, I am fifteen weeks and will need to have the surgical abortion. This is a small operation of a vacuum suction under general anaesthetic where the medical team will open up my cervix to enable the hand-held suction device to empty my womb.

I then get shown into a cubicle to get changed and put a hospital gown on, it's open at the back; I also slip on some disposable knickers with a large sanitary towel attached. I'm holding back the tears as hard as I can, hoping she'll call me in quickly, so I can get it over and done with. The nurse comes in and asks, "Are you ready?"

I nod my head and follow her through to another room in which I climb on the bed. As I'd remembered it looked like a hospital, bright lights, a medical team, some on chairs sitting at the bottom of my bed with masks covering their mouths and plastic gloves on. I have an anaesthetist standing next to me, she explains that she's going to give me some anaesthetic and it's going to feel cold. She slowly pushes it through my hand, as it travels through my veins, I start to count to three, I can feel the icy cold liquid running through my veins one...two... I didn't get to three.

I wake up in another room still laying on the bed. I feel violated and empty. I know it's gone. A piece of toast with tea lays on the table next to me. In a drowsy state, I try to sit myself up tenderly touching my stomach. I want to bawl so hard right now, but I just need to get my ass out this place and home. The blood I can sense is filling the sanitary towel. I allowed them to suck my baby into a clinical vacuum and now I'm left with the aftermath in these disposable thingy's. What kind of person am I? When I first got this procedure done I was certain that it was my step dad's so there was no question about, what I needed to do. I felt physically sick at the thought of him growing inside of me. This time, it was different, I was older and knew it wasn't right, I didn't have a genuine reason to dispose of this life.

I'm supposed to be accompanied home, but I just don't care right now, I just need to go. I call a taxi and gently get my clothes back on.

When I finally get home, to my disappointment Paul is there sitting on the sofa in the living room, and Kayla is in her room, as I peep around the door say hello and ask her how school was. I look around, but our son is not home, so I ask Paul, "Where is he?"

"He's at nursery," he replied.

"Well can you get him please?" I ask.

"Nope, I'm about roll myself a spliff and chill."

"He needs to be picked up Paul and I don't have the energy right now."

"Well neither do I. If he needs to be picked up so badly, you'll find yourself some!"

I stand there speechless, staring at him. In the pain I'm in, I just shake my head in disgust. It was like what I had to endure wasn't enough.

"Well you're going to be late if you don't get a move on," he says looking at me, like why am I still standing there.

I leave the house and walk up to the nursery, feeling all types of emotions. I ring the bell as I do, and wait for one of the workers to come and let me in.

"Hi, I've come to pick up Paul Jnr."

"Let me go get him for you," the worker answers.

"Thank you," I reply as she goes to. him.

As she returns him to me, she asks if I'm okay, as she looks down on the floor to between my legs. I'm leaking.

"Oh... I've... Just found out I had a miscarriage," I say ashamed with myself.

"Sorry to hear," was the workers response.

"Can I use the toilet please?" I ask.

"Sure," the worker says pointing to where it is.

As I try to tidy myself as much as I can, I ring a taxi to pick us up. As close as we were, I feel that the flow is too heavy, and I don't even know if I'll even make it home with the combination of the pain and not eating all day.

The taxi comes and Paul Jnr. and I get in and reach home in a matter of minutes.

I come back in the flat and all is unusually quiet and I'm unsure why. Paul was chilling before I left, playing his game. Something didn't seem right. I put our son in my room in his cot, to see where Paul was.

I think forget if Paul's in the house? If he has left me good ridents, instead I check if Kayla is in her room and okay. I slowly push open her door, but not prepared for what I discover, and that was my baby girl touching Paul in the mid-width area and he too was touching in hers.

His eyes catch mine with the dirtiest smirk on his face. I scream nooooooooooooo noooooooooooo noooooooooooooooooo GET OFF HER NOW!!! As I see red, my hands stretch out in front of me, and I go straight for his neck. He laughs as he squeezes my arms to try and loosen my grip. I'm struggling to get out of his clutch, so I kick him, spit in his face, this angers him, so still holding onto my arms he swings me and hits my head off the chest of drawers. I then with the little strength I have, kick him back in his groin and he jumps off me.

Kayla screams, "Mummy no!"

I scream back, "Kayla go to your brother and shut the door," as Paul hurls himself back towards me.

Kayla runs out the room crying, I should go after her, but I'm not letting this guy get away with this and I need answers.

"Why Paul? Why! She is your daughter!"

"Don't need to play stupid no more. I know you really don't believe I thought she was my child for all these years?" He sniggers.

"You think I'm stupid? Got me looking after another man's child and you thought I'd be okay with that? You didn't think I'd find out? Your stepfather told me that you were seeing someone else and you were playing me, before Kayla was born. I didn't believe him at first but once she was born and she didn't have the same blood type of me or you, I knew it."

"That still doesn't explain why you would do what you did, to a child and one that saw you as her father. You are sick!"

"Well, at the time it felt right, and you haven't been giving me much attention lately, you've been either doing Uni work or working at the bar and she's been here with me tending to my needs in your absence. Maybe you should have got your priorities straight and this may never have happened."

My arm swings back and smacks him straight in the jaw.

"How dare you?" I scream.

Holding his jaw and realising that I had caused blood to disperse from his mouth. He wipes his mouth and says whilst pointing and looking straight into my eyes, "I'll give you that one for free."

I glare back at him, "This does not make any sense, you have continued to live here knowing the truth, not saying anything and at no point did you try and walk away. Kayla did not need to get caught up in any of this."

"Well I had nowhere else to go, dummy. The whole set up was convenient for me."

"I thought you loved me Paul?"

"Nah. I never loved you, I just wanted to get in your knickers and then one thing after another happened. My mum kicked me out, you became pregnant, I made use of my bad situation and worked it to my advantage... You thought I really wanted you didn't you? Me, want you? I pitied you?"

In a state of crying, and feeling angry, I yell, "How could you?"

He laughs again. I say, "What is so funny? Why do you keep laughing?"

He continues to laugh, "... It's because you're a joke!"

I just can't hold it in no more, I pull out one of the drawers and I whack it across his head. I'm finding anything in my reach I can hit him with, the lamp, the books. He's hitting me back with his fists a lot harder than what I'm discharging, I can feel each connect of his hand to my face, but as I fight back, the pain I'm supposed to feel, fades leaving me numb. All that I've done for him, the time I'd wasted, allowed him to be under the same roof as my baby girl and.... and.... so many images are going through my mind then he gives me one last blow and I drop to the floor.

As I lay there motionless, my vision's blurry, I can see Paul walk away. I can hear my babies screaming but I'm in such a daze I don't even know what's happening right now.

I am unaware how long I must have been out cold for, but I can hear a persistent knocking at the door. I drag myself along the floor, my arm hugging my ribs taking each movement slow, to try reach the front door. As I pull myself up the wall to grab the latch, I finally get to it, as the door opens, it's the police. Two of them.

"We've been called as neighbours believe there was a disturbance?" says the female police officer.

I don't respond I'm just standing there. He's talking but it's like my ears are absorbing the words but there's no sound.

"Miss is everything ok?" The male officer asks.

I still remain non-responsive.

The male police officer, then puts his hand on my door ready to push it, "I think it's best we come in," he says. I permit him to enter my home with no hesitation, I have no fight left in me.

I'm standing there, God knows what my face looks like, bloodied up, just like my trousers that had soaked through from when I was at the nursery. What must they be thinking right now?

They walk around the flat inspecting each room, recording their findings of the broken furniture, discarded blood, transferred on various items.

I then hear the police officers say, as they open my bedroom door, and witnessed, Kayla huddling Paul Jnr. in her arms on the bed;

"We're going to need social services, there are kids here," he spoke into his walkie talkie.

"What? Why? You can't take my kids. You can't. Listen to me please."

I make my way to the kids, grabbing them, holding them one in each arm accompanying them on the bed. I'm pleading with the officers, crying, shaking. If I could see myself, I probably didn't appear like, I could care after myself let alone them, but that wasn't the case.

"Who did this to you? Partner? Ex-partner?" the female officer asks.

I didn't want to respond I'm just thinking what are they going to do with my kids?

"It's in your best interest that you cooperate with us, so we can get a better idea of the situation and support you appropriately," she continues.

I remain unhelpful, I don't need or want their help. I just wished that I could rewind all events from today, to the day I met Paul. In no way did I regret my son, I just wished things were different. If I thought that way, I'd be rewinding time, from the first time my stepdad touched me and then I'd not have Kayla. These were the cards I was dealt, and I needed to handle them, no regrets just know what I was going to do, to ensure I moved forward, hopeful for the future.

The social workers soon came and I'm holding my babies as tight as I can, not knowing when I'll next be able to see them. The social worker speaks, "This is just not a suitable environment for them right now. It's not that you won't be able to see them, it's just temporary until you get yourself sorted."

I say ok, by nodding my head. I need to clean up this place, clean myself up. What must my kids be thinking seeing mummy's face like this?

I kiss them both on the forehead and say, "I love you. Mummy will always love you. Make sure you look out for each other."

They say, "Love you too mummy," and start to walk away from me out the door. Kayla looked back waving as she would, when we'd say our goodbyes in the morning at school. This time with a solemn face and tears in her eyes. When they're out of sight and ear shot, I drop down to my knees and I cry, and I cry, and I cry. "My babies, I need my babies."

The female officer says, "We've called an ambulance they'll be here to take you to the hospital to get you checked over."

The officers wait with me until the Paramedics arrive, a stretcher gets rolled in and I'm laid out on it. The Paramedic gets her blood pressure monitor out to put the inflatable cuff on my arm, she asks me, "What is your name? Can you hear me?"

She shines her pen torch in my eyes to see if I can follow the light. She explains she needs to remove my upper body clothing to check for injuries, bruising or bleeding. She asks, "Is there any medication you're currently taking at the moment,"

I shake my head, "No."

"Are you allergic to any medication that you're aware of?" I shake my head, "No."

"Are you pregnant?"

I say, "Not anymore." That's the last I remember as an oxygen mask is put over my nose and mouth, and I am transferred into the ambulance.

The next time I open my eyes, I'm conscious, I'm in a hospital bed. I must have had a deep sleep as I'm on a ward, cleaned up, in a gown with a new sanitary towel on. Everything's a blur, so much time I can't account for.

A nurse comes to my bed to assess me, check how I'm feeling, if I need any extra blankets or sanitary towels. As she props me up with the pillows and makes me more comfortable in bed, she gives me a menu to choose something for lunch and dinner. She tells me to choose now, so that she can give it to the kitchen. Before she walks away she tells me a lady regularly visits these wards for referrals of women who potentially may have been a victim of domestic violence. She relays that, if I want to talk to someone, she will be around shortly. I say, "Thank you," and she smiles, along with, "That's what I'm here for."

I'm lying in my bed, not thinking about anything, gazing into space for a substantial period of time, when I hear someone say, "Hello, would you like me to come back?"

As I shake off the mini trance I'm in, I reply, "Sorry I was in another world, what is it you wanted?"

"I'm Coleen and I run a women's organisation called Y.A.N.A that helps women such as yourself, that may be tackling different issues and unsure of where to get help."

"Oh yeah, the nurse said you'd be round. I'm not up for talking right now, I'm still in shock and can't fathom complete sentences right now."

"Not to worry, I'll leave you with our pamphlet for you to look at in your own time. When you're ready, come to our Centre and meet some of our other ladies. It's not all doom and gloom we do have a laugh too."

"Okay thanks, I'll definately keep this in mind," taking it out her hand.

"My number is also on there if you want to talk at any time."

I smile, "Thank you," and she walks away.

Coleen was very friendly, and she brought me this sense of belief that there was a silver lining, she had a genuine aura about her. She dressed conventional, though she appeared young in age. Her hair was natural, no chemical, nor heat seemed to of ever touched it. It was really nice how she had it in guinea twists tied up into one. She also had deep, clear, ebony skin to suit her oval shaped face and though small black eyes, they stood out white like snow. I was curious about what her story was and how she began her path on helping women in need.

A couple of days had passed, and I was healing satisfactorily enough, to be able to go home. I had no visitors, as I was not on talking terms with my so-called birth mother. My friends I used to have distanced themselves from me whilst I was with Paul, for my refusal to listen to them when they said he was no good for me. I was at the point I needed someone now. I didn't even have the kids around for comfort.

I thought, and I thought who I could call. I rummaged in my bag and saw the business card. Daphne?.... Caroline? Whatever she calls herself. Should I call her? Do I want her here? Won't she judge me? I don't care I've got nothing else to lose. I dial the numbers and it starts to ring... RING RING RING... RING RING RING... RING RING RING... RING RING RING... As I'm about to put the phone down, the phone is picked up.

"Hello this is Daphne; how can I be of service to you?"

"Hello, can I speak to Caroline?"

"Whom may I ask is speaking?"

"It's Celine, you gave me your card and told me to call."

"Ooooooh, it's Caroline. Hey Hun, you decided you want to work with me then?"

"Not exactly, I wanted to know if it's possible for you to come and see me, I'm in the hospital at the moment?"

"Okay, nothing too serious I hope?"

"Well... Nah, nah, I'm on the mend now, it'll just be nice to have someone here if you don't mind being that person."

"Alright, what hospital you in?"

"City Hospital on the Stanley Road?"

"Yeah I know it. See you shortly."

"Thank you," and I end the call.

I didn't expect for her to be at all receptive, she didn't know me, but she was willing to come to my aid.

It takes her no more than an hour to arrive, and as she did when I first met her, strutted herself through the ward to my bed. As I watched her I could also see the surrounding patients watching her too, like who is she? It was hard not to see her as we could hear the sound of her heels going click clack on the hospital floor. I laughed once she reached me.

"What is everyone staring at?" Caroline says confusingly.

"They probably think you're a super model," I say trying to humour her.

"I guess so," she said feeling herself, patting her hair. As she realised why she actually was here, she looked at me and said, "Oh my God Hun. Look at you! Who did this?"

"My partner, ex-partner now I should say."

"No way. How could he do this? Where's your kids?"

"They've been taken off me," I flood into tears.

"Oh my gosh... Okay we need to sort you out. I met you less than a week ago and all I see is... this," as she looks me up and down and moves her hand around.

"You're coming with me. I've brought you some clothes to change into and a few little female condiments as I was unsure what you had."

I smile, "Thank you, it really means a lot."

"Hurry up and get changed, time is money, and we need to get you back in ship shape, so you can come work with me."

"I don't know, I don't think that's for me."

"Well how else you going to get yourself back to normality and repair your home for the kids to come back to?"

I didn't want to say it out loud, but she was right.

THE OTHER HALF

When I got changed, I asked the nurse if I was able to be discharged. She went to ask the doctor his opinion and returned to state that there were no concerns with my health, so they discharged me, and both me and Caroline walked out of hospital.

I was wearing her shades to shield my black eyes and bruised face. I felt like I was her, walking in her clothes, this wasn't my usual attire. We walked through the car park to get to where she parked the car. She had a cute two-seater Mercedes AMG, I put my bags in the boot and carefully climbed into the passenger seat (I still felt fragile). It felt surreal, I'd never experienced this in my life, a life of luxury if you'd call it that. I hadn't got the wealth, but I was able to get an idea of what it may feel like.

As we drove towards Caroline's house, passing through the parts of Baringham I knew, I started to admire the surroundings and areas I was unfamiliar with which were breathtaking; the lawns mown, the beautiful flower beds, clean brickwork of the house's exterior. I loved to see the detail on a property. That's what I wanted to do, what I was studying for. There was so much inspiration to take in around me of what I could potentially be aiming towards career wise. For once in my life I felt free and positive, everything may work out for me and the kids.

We were an hour into our journey, Caroline informed me that we were close now, we just needed to go further through the lanes. We hadn't spoken too much in the car, I presume Caroline thought I may need some head space. I couldn't shrug off how nice Caroline had been to me, I've not had anyone come to my rescue like that, although I know there were some obvious ulterior motives. I was glad not to be stuck in the hospital or in an empty flat alone.

We eventually pulled up to her house, let me rephrase, 'manor'. It was electric gated with metal fencing all around, white stoned driveway, a triple garage with parking for up to five vehicles and a fountain as a Centre piece. As she used her electronic fob on the side of the gate, it automatically opened. Wow... It was amazing, I couldn't wait to go inside. I'd never experienced anything like this before, so the smallest thing was amazing to me right now.

We parked up the car and walked up towards the double oak doors of the front entrance to the manor. As she opened them it revealed an extensive marbled reception hall, that branched off to entrances of other rooms to the sides and middle of it and a dual staircase which was the focal point.

You could tell that it had been refurbished to look contemporary, but the detail was kept from the exposed ceiling beams or renaissance styled painted ceilings reserving it's traditional style. As I was given a tour of over three floors, I noticed at least five bedrooms with en-suites, a dining room, drawing room, sitting room, all with feature fireplaces, indoor swimming pool overlooking the two acres of gardens pleasantly decorated with a variety of flowers, orchard of pears and apples and a two storey cottage detached from the main house.

The comparison of my two bed flat I lived in, in an eight storey council block named the worst in Baringham was menial to this. Our lifestyle was on two different levels, I definitely was able to see, this is how the other half lived.

When we got to Caroline's bedroom, (which was on what she informed me was the east wing), it was all I imagined a princess to have. The furniture was in antique white with detailed carvings to add a classic touch, from the queen size four poster bed supported by a metal canopy, a night stand, dresser and mirror. The heavily draped curtains and champagne coloured vintage rug complimented the style of the room. The hidden gem of the room was the partitioned side which looked like a wall of mirrors. As you slid the doors open from the middle you were taken by surprise of a walk-in wardrobe, built from floor to ceiling, including storage compartments sectioned for each type of clothing; shoes, shirts, dresses, slide out trouser racks, top shelves for hat boxes, slide out drawers for jewellery to be neatly displayed and brightly lit with installed spotlights.

"You okay Celine?" Caroline asked me.

"Yeah, yeah, yeah. Just overwhelmed I guess by the way you live," I replied.

"It's not as great as it seems. I had it all, but I spent most of my time here alone, whilst my mum spent her nights out the house. It wasn't fun at all."

"I know what you mean, I didn't spend much time with my mother either growing up, she left me in the house whilst she went to work, and I stayed with my stepfather. He used to abuse me every time she was AWOL. My earliest memory as a child was trying to stop her from leaving the house by barricading the door and be as adamant as I could be, that I wanted her to stay at home with me and not go to work. It was no use, she used to push me away and say, "Stop it! I don't have time for this." As I got older, I just didn't do anything, I just anticipated that as the door shut my stepfather would be not too far, waiting for me. I tried to fight back at times, but as he was always stronger than me, he'd win and then make sure I felt him even more, to ensure I didn't act up next time. I'd be bruised down below and be bleeding, to the point it stung whilst I peed, or knickers rubbed against my skin. I had to get a cold damp flannel, to pat against my skin or sit in a bath of cold water so that it felt soothed."

"So, did you end up telling your mum what happened?"

"Yeah, I did when I was 16 and started having a boyfriend."

"And what did she say?"

"She slapped me in the face and said I don't want to hear that sort of nastiness come from your mouth. Don't make me have to wash your mouth out with soap and water. Look how much he's done for us and you want to tell lies, you know where liars go? Hell! And that's exactly where you'll be heading if I hear those words come out of your mouth again."

"That's horrible," Caroline commented sympathetically.

"I've just attempted to block that part of my life out of my head... My stepfather later tried to say when my mother came in one night and caught us on the settee together that I tried to make a move on him, even though I hadn't. I got kicked out that night, was pregnant too but she didn't know at this point."

"No way, I don't know how you've been able to carry on, have kids and try to strive on having a normal life."

"I had to, there was no space for doubt in my mind or I can't, as my kids depended on me. There was no other choice."

"I don't know what to say... Now you're being abused in a different way but, by your boyfriend!"

"F@%* me being abused! The reason I ended up in hospital was I fought him, as I walked in on him abusing my daughter... I just don't know how come I couldn't see the signs? The cycle has come back round on my offspring!"

"He was her dad, there would be no way of you knowing," Caroline said trying to console me.

"He stated when we were arguing that night, that he always knew she wasn't his, but didn't disclose it as it benefited him being in my home."

"Sick! Absolutely sick! He's locked up now right?"

"I can't answer that question, as I don't know. He left me on the floor bloody as he fled the house, leaving me with the kids bawling and the police finding me in that state. That's the reason why the social workers came and took them from me."

"We're going to get the best lawyers and we're going to fight this. He's not going to get away with this."

"These men always do though, don't they? Look at my stepfather, still with my so-called birth mother, living happily in their house, knowing full well what happened year upon year."

"I'm not prepared to do nothing. It's better to try and do something and get some result... I'm sorry you had to endure all of that, makes me feel like I shouldn't complain at all about my life."

"Why you sorry for? You didn't do anything, you didn't know me. I don't want your pity, it's not why I told you."

Caroline shakes her head, putting it down with dismay. I can tell she is upset by what I have told her from the sniffling and discreet hand wipes of her eyes.

I tried to lighten up the mood, "Come on you were telling me earlier about my face. Don't make my problems transfer unto you, snap out of it."

We then hear a voice shout out, "Caroline... Caroline...."

"That'll be my Mum," as she tries to make herself presentable.

The door knocks. "Come in Mum," Caroline says.

Her Mum opens the door, "Oh, hello."

I could tell she was a little taken back that I was there.

"You never told me, you were having a friend over tonight," she said.

"Neither did I, but I do now," Caroline says sternly.

"Well I was hoping we would all have dinner tonight."

"What! Me, you, Gran and Granddad?"

"Yes," her Mother replied.

"Well now Celine will be joining us."

"I don't know if that'll be a good idea Caroline."

"Why wouldn't it be?"

"Don't say I didn't warn you. You know what your Granddad's like."

"I couldn't care less what he thinks right now."

"Whilst your still under this house, you will respect him, whether you like it or not. See you in the dining room in an hour." As she starts to walk towards the door, she turns to me, "It was nice to meet you Celine, sorry about that."

"No worries. It was nice to meet you too."

As Caroline's Mum closes the door behind her, Caroline in frustration says,

"Eurgh, they annoy me. I don't know why they still attempt to persist in these dinners when there's no connection."

"Well, as you said, it's better to try than not at all."

You should have seen the look of disapproval come on Caroline's face, she was not impressed by my response.

"Wait till dinner, and then you'll soon understand."

We both had a shower and got dressed for dinner. I was unsure of what to expect at dinner, with Caroline's opinion on her grandfather being outspoken with his thoughts. I'd never gone to a friend's home before, the insignificant being didn't agree with visiting anyone other than our family's home, so it wouldn't become a habit. She'd say, "Never get too comfortable in someone else's home, more than your own."

I didn't want to embarrass Caroline in any way, or feel awkward being in their presence I guess, all I could was try my best.

"You ready to go down?" Caroline said.

"Yeah," I said.

"Come on, let's get this over and done with."

As we head down the staircase, the dining room doors were open, and you could hear the mild sound of talking.

As we walk in Caroline's Gran says, "Caroline, where have you been my dear?"

"Working hard Gran," she says as she kisses her from cheek to cheek.

She moves towards her Granddad's seat at the head of the table, to kiss him on the cheek and he's staring at me.

"Caroline."

"Yes, Granddad."

"What's a n****! doing coming to dine at my dinner table?"

"Grandad can you be polite to my friend please?" Caroline asked nicely.

"I will have no one tell me what to do, now answer the question Caroline."

53

Before she could answer. I speak, "Sir, if you'd prefer for me not to dine at your table then I understand, but as a guest, trying to remain as polite as possible, I'd like you to correct your language when you address me, as I am not a n****!"

"You are, and that's the last I'm going to say on the matter. If you want to continue this meal you won't respond to me further."

I could tell Caroline was embarrassed right now and so was I for her. I didn't expect that kind of welcome. He thought he was reasonable by saying what he did, and that he was up to par. Who am I to come into his home and say otherwise, if that's the way he was brought up?

Caroline later told me, that her Granddad was old skool, brought up at a time when couldn't see past colour. It wasn't natural for him to see black people mix in the same social functions, circles, work environments as white people. It wasn't that he had a direct racist hatred towards black people, he'd just rather not communicate with them. He hadn't ever said anything directly against Caroline she'd later say, but maybe he had convinced himself she was just like him, white.

The table was nicely prepared with ample amount of food to go around.

Caroline's Gran asked me, "Are you enjoying your dinner?"

"Yes, thank you it is very nice," I replied.

"I'm glad you like it dear."

"We've got things to be doing, so we won't be here for coffee and cheese biscuits," Caroline firmly states.

"Caroline, we don't do this often, so if it's just once a week, make the effort please," her Mum said.

She agrees to disagree and so we stay for coffee and cheese biscuits.

When we finish, I say, "Thank you all for your hospitality," to those around the table and tuck in my chair.

Caroline's Gran replies, "You're welcome dear," and we head back up the stairs to Caroline's room.

We couldn't get back any quicker to Caroline's room, dinner was so uncomfortable.

"I'm so glad that's over. Sorry you had to sit through that," Caroline said, relieved we were back in her room relaxing.

"Don't worry about it. What I don't understand is, can't he see that you are partly black too? If he's calling me a n****, he's calling you one too?"

"I don't know what he thinks, never have, he's not shared those feelings with me and I've not wished to probe him, just in case, I didn't get the response I desired.

"Okay ladies, that was a very intense session you had to absorb. We are going to take a small break and resume in an hour. In this time, you can help yourself to the refreshments provided and have a look at the worksheets in your pack until we reconvene. Thank you for your participation so far," says Caroline ending the first part of the session in Hall 1.

A.W.W CONVENTION WORKSHEETS

REVELATION

What are your main goals for reading this book? What do you expect on completion?

…..

…..

…..

…..

…..

…..

What is your interpretation on the meaning of 'a womans worth?'

…..

…..

…..

…..

…..

What has happened in your past that you have not been able to get over?

....

....

....

....

....

....

Task: Write about it and throw it away, burn etc. And note to self to forgive. Express your feelings in this piece of writing

_____

What do you feel at the moment you're under pressure with?

....

....

....

....

....

How do you think you could be honest with yourself to feel freer from this pressure?

…...

…...

....

…..

....

Do you believe there is anything hindering your growth that you need to fight off at this current time, so you can move forward?

…..

…..

....

…...

....

Do you believe you have an addiction?

…...

Do you want / need help?

If you answered yes. Go to help me pages at the back of the book

TREAD WITH CAUTION

Have you ever been abused in any way before? Sexually/ Physically/ Mentally/ Emotionally?

How did you feel? Create word clouds for your feelings? Did you tell anyone? If you did, their reaction? If not, why not?

....

....

....

....

....

....

Have you got a decision to make but you don't know what to choose? Write down the pros and cons. These need to be your choices

....

....

....

....

. . . .

. . . .

. . . .

. . . .

Freedom To Speak

If you could share a story about yourself and get advice on what it was, what would it be

. . . .

. . . .

. . . .

. . . .

. . . .

. . . .

. . . .

. . . .

. . . .

. . . .

. . . .

SECRET BLACKIE

Welcome back ladies, I hope we are all feeling refreshed after our break and ready to move on to the second part of our session. I hope it's got your minds thinking about your own situations and how you can conquer all the burdens that are trying to keep you down," Caroline delivers to the audience of participants in the session in Hall 1 with Kayla.

"Now to continue on with my story, which is connected with the life of the late Celine, I will talk about my viewpoint to what happened next," Caroline continues.

As we get comfortable lying on the bed, I ask Celine, "Can I ask you a question?"

"Yeah sure," Celine replies.

"Can you tell me what's it like being black?"

"In what way?" she asks.

"I don't know, anything. What do you use in your hair? What kind of foods do you eat? What do they taste like? What's the story with Martin Luther King? Why did he have a dream? Show me how to twerk this ass of mine," I laugh.

"I want to know everything. I've been sheltered in every aspect of black culture and that's half the contribution that makes up who I am. When I saw you in the clinic, part of me was intrigued to get to know you as there was no one else there. This gave me a little reassurance that if you were likely to brush me off, it would've been less embarrassing. When you called me, I was happy, thought this was my way to conjure up the courage to get to know you, and know who I was in some strange way.

When I was young, I went to an all-girls school which was predominantly white, you could tell that I was different and didn't fit in regardless of the amount of wealth my family owned or gave towards donations to extra curriculum activities for the school.

The kids used to bully me, they did not include me in games at playtime. They would call me names like secret blackie or bleached at birth. I was a loner, unable to connect with my peers on a mutual level or have someone accessible to confide in, on how I was feeling. I tried to tell my Mother and she'd say to ignore them, they're talking nonsense, you're beautiful, few sticks and stones darling. She was unable to relate with me on any level whilst growing up, she was constantly in and out of the house with new conquests and let's not bring in my Grandparents. Getting any attention from Granddad was like drawing water from a stone and Gran's communication was a little tap on the back with a, "Here, here, dear don't you worry, things will sort itself out," but they never.

When it was dinnertime at school, I felt like everyone was watching me, I used to bring in my own lunch and hide in a classroom or a quiet place where no one saw me and then afterwards I'd get this urge to regurgitate it all back up. I maintained this cycle at home after tea; go to the bathroom put my fingers down my throat, gag to get it back up to then going to the kitchen and stocking my room up with crisps, chocolates and any other junk I could find. I did this up to leaving school and no one at the time noticed my weight fluctuating, or my change of moods, I was left to my own device to fend for myself.

I started losing these urges as I started to get attention from men at work at my first little job as a receptionist at this Grade II listed hotel retreat a few miles away from my home. The visitors were very wealthy men, business like, would stare at me and give little friendly gestures when I checked them in or gave them mini tours of our facilities there. I had business cards slipped to me on many occasions but didn't do anything with them. My Granddad would have killed me, if he found out. He knew the owner and giving me a job was a favour, so couldn't give any reason to bring shame on the family for my ignorance. It made me start to pay attention to my appearance though. They complimented me on the features that I would have got teased about like my bottom and my lips. I started to embrace them by purchasing fitted trousers and lipsticks. I gradually then explored video tutorials of how you do makeup by going to beauty store counters and observing how and what they were doing to my face. I soon became an expert at it and accumulated a pretty good makeup collection of almost every brand, in different shades, from the eyeshadows to the lippies.

Whilst working part time, I then convinced my Grandparents to pay for me to go beauty school where I met my first boyfriend. His name was Mark. He came from a good family background, played football for our county and was very popular within the community. We were dating for quite a while, but it was nowhere near a healthy relationship. He started commenting on the way I looked and said I was gaining weight so the binge eating returned. I enjoyed eating and there was always a gala dinner or an awards ceremony we had to attend, so after I ate our four-course meal, I'd find somewhere I could throw up. When I didn't have admittance to go in the gardens at the venue, I'd find a vase to do it in. In addition to this, Mark and his friends were accustomed to taking lines of coke. I soon joined in once, the other girlfriends told me, we all do it, and how it would help keep off the calories, so I thought let's roll with it, should be harmless and if it'll help me keep off some pounds, why not.

I was wrong to believe it would be that easy, the come downs were the worse but I continued to consume it, to keep me high. Mark and I had a regime of doing it before sex, to make him more arrogant than he already was, and so he could last a little longer, as he was always premature. Yeah, I lost my virginity with Mark. Mark was just the beginning of my rollercoaster lifestyle but as I had no financial commitments and thrived on a busy social life, I didn't care. I began to hear rumours that Mark was cheating on me, I confronted him, and he got aggressive, shouting at me and said after all he'd done for me, why would he do that.

He'd calm down and say he loved me, 'Don't worry babe, you're the only one for me,' and slap my ass with a comment, 'But I think you should lose a little of that ass though babe it's getting big again."

One day after a seven-day binge eating, being sick, grams and grams of coke, I came to Mark's place to unload. I let myself in, and as I made my way up the stairs, down the corridor, towards his bedroom, I saw a girl walking from his en suite bathroom, I'd recognised her as she'd started hanging out at the football club.

She looked at me and said, "What the hell?!"

"I'm his girlfriend you silly bitch," I said. I then heard Mark coming from behind me saying, "I've got the bottle on ice baby." As he reached me, he said unnervingly, "You're just in time baby, might as well join in the party and have some fun."

I was angry and knocked the bottle out his hand, with the bucket of ice dropping to the floor.

He shouted, "What the f@%* you doing?"

With me responding, "How could you do this to me?"

As I'm trying to hit him, crying my eyes out, he's restraining my wrists, so I can't move. He says, "I think it's best you go now fatty, this relationship has run its course," as he shoves me out the bedroom doorway and closes the door. I hear him say, "So, where were we?" to the skank, as she giggles, and I stagger down the stairs knocking each photo with my hand on the wall to the ground.

I'm unsure how I got home, all I know is that when I eventually woke up, the first thing I wanted to see was the toilet bowl, so I could throw up. A perfect comedown, head banging, mouth dry as f@%! I needed some coke, but I didn't have any, so I went back to bed to sleep it off. Next day came, and my mum comes in, "What the hell happened to you? Not heard a peak out of you for a couple of days. Work called I covered for you, said that you've got a terrible flu and that you'll be in touch when you're on the mend."

"Thanks," I said in my rough morning voice.

"No problem sweetie, I'll get you a cup of tea, and you'll be right as rain in no time."

She was right, I jumped in the shower, washed my hair and had a cuppa, feeling like who's Mark? Let's get the ball rolling, fresh new day, fresh start. So, I called work and queried if they needed any help, and they said they did, so off I went.

I could tell from waking up that morning that everything was going to be different and it was. A gentleman came to the reception counter whilst I was trying to reacquaint myself with my work duties and said, "Can I book myself in for the night?"

I popped up from the desk startled and said, "Of course sir. What type of room would you require?"

He said, "Have you got anything close to a presidential suite?"

I said, "One moment," tapping on the computer keyboard to check.

"Let me see if it's available?... It is sir, would you like me to go ahead and book?"

"Yes," taking out his card from his wallet to put in the card machine.

As we wait for payment to go through, which it does, I give him his receipt, and come from around the reception desk to direct him to his room, leaving reception unmanned.

The presidential suite was the best of the best, at the hotel it was like a palatial apartment situated on two floors. It had a spiral staircase located in the middle of the spacious lounge area, opposite a kitchen and separate dining section. On the next level it was comprised of two bedrooms, containing a super king-size bed and other a queen-sized bed, an en-suite bathroom for each, one containing a sunken whirlpool bath the other freestanding with overhead shower, bidets, private sauna and hot tub on one of three balconies that oversees the acres of land. It was elegant, immaculately designed from all aspects of the ceilings, covings, doorways and staircase bannister.

As we got to the door and I opened it, we entered inside, me ushering him in first, to explain about facilities and if he had any problems who and how to get help. He responded with saying, "How am I able to have you for the night?"

"Pardon?" I replied taken back.

"I'll pay you of course... How does a grand for the night in cash sound?"

I was a bit taken back by his proposal, I had never been offered such a proposition, but was intrigued into what that would entail to spend a night in the presidential suite with him. He gave me his business card, as I stood there pro-founded, and said to me, "Well give me a call if you're up for it, would love to show a beautiful lady such as yourself a good time."

"Okay, thanks," putting the card in my shirt pocket, closing the door and heading back to reception.

As I reached back, sitting at my station behind the reception desk, it was all I could think about. A grand for the night. He wasn't even too bad looking, though he was in his late 40s. He was Caucasian but smooth tanned skin as though he lived in the sun, crystal blue eyes, dark shaven hair and a husky beard which gave him this rugged look though he dressed in bespoke attire. I came to the conclusion, why not?

I finished work at 7pm so went home to pack an overnight bag of toiletries, underwear and nightwear. I called him and said I'd have a shower and be with him for half 8. He said that would be perfect and looked forward to it.

When I got there, I tried my best to avoid any of my colleagues on the way to his room. I knocked on the door and he opened it in one of our hotel white robes. He ushered me in and gave me a glass of bubbly that was already poured. He kissed my cheek and said you look amazing. Let me take your coat, so you can get comfortable. He took my coat and hung it up, when he came back, he said first things first let me give you this, handing me an envelope. "It's all there but you can check it if you need to," he told me.

"I've never done this before, so it's new to me," I responded.

"Just relax I won't make you do anything you don't want to. I've been working tremendously lately and I'm just in need of some good female company."

I nodded with okay and sat on the chaise lounge to take off my shoes.

We talked on the sofa for a while facing each other. He told me to lift up my legs to rest them on him as he massaged them. It felt so good as I lay my head back and closed my eyes. I was relaxed he was pressing all the correct pressure points in my feet. As he slowed down to stop, I could feel his hand stroking up my leg, as he started to move his head up my chest to my neck kissing it. It was sensual whilst ticklish as his grizzly beard brushed against my skin. His lips finally reached mine as we passionately kissed, our arms wrapped around each other's bodies and my legs crossed around his back, so we were clutched tightly together, entwined like a ball of string. He knew exactly what to do, to arouse me, he picked me up and carried me up the staircase and placed me on the king-size bed, undressing me slowing kissing my thighs and torso on each movement. When I was fully unclothed, he gently climbed on top of me and put himself inside of me, each thrust, made me moan and groan...

"Okay, okay, okay, I get the picture, too much detail, get to the point," Celine rudely interrupted.

"Alright I was just giving you an image," I tried to explain to her.

"Too much information, where is this story heading?" Celine said to hurry me up.

"Okay so, the night of passion ended but Ray and I, (that was his name), began to frequently meet up. He took me places I never thought of going, each time insistent that he should pay me, whether it was for a night, a day, weekend, or week. I actually enjoyed spending time with him, I was able to see this whole other world that enlightened my perspective. It then dried up as he became very clingy as if I belonged to him. It wasn't supposed to be like that, so I moved on.

As I had got the exposure of this new life, I wanted more so I decided to produce my own business cards, go to exclusive places slip certain men my card and then that's how I became, Daphne.

"No way. So, do you sleep with all your clients?" Celine asked me.

"Oh no. It all depends on each individual, mostly I just escort them to functions, give them a dance in their home or a blow job. I do have rules and expectations of them before we meet, that I go through with them on the phone."

"So how come you became pregnant, you were, weren't you? That's why we both ended up meeting in an abortion clinic?"

"I had rekindled my contact with Ray. He is the only person I'd slept with unprotected as we have an understanding with each other. He was in the area and we got a bit wild and with the consumption of alcohol and being on antibiotics it cancelled the pill out I suppose."

Celine shakes her head.

"What's that shake of disapproval for?" I ask her.

"It's a dangerous business, you could really get yourself in a compromising situation."

"Well so far so good, and with my new partner in crime, you that is, I should be fine."

"What have I got myself into?" she says.

"Into what? It will be the best decision you make, to get you back on track."

"If you say so."

"Yes, I do," with a big grin on my face and a pout of the mouth to her direction.

I chatted with Celine to the early hours. We watched different movies she grew up on; like The Color Purple, Waiting to Exhale, whilst she cornrowed my hair into two, and munched on popcorn. I felt so comfortable around her, it was like having a sister I never had. As we spoke, her demeanor rubbed off on me, to the point I wanted my mum to tell me more about my father and his family. I'd missed out on so much already as a child. On reflection I believe this has possibly prevented me from achieving my full potential and being the best version of me.

FREEDOM TO SPEAK

The next day Celine had our day planned out, she said that this would be the start of our journey to healing from the experiences we had encountered so far in this entity called life. She explained how she'd met Coleen in hospital after recent events, and how she had an organisation where we could talk and hear about other women's experiences.

I agreed that I'd accompany her there, as I wanted to support her on the path to recovery. We directed ourselves to the address that was on the pamphlet she was given, and it wasn't too hard to find. The building didn't stand out from the outside, to bring too much attention to what was inside, but when you went inside it was very welcoming. It had beautiful paintings that must have been done by artists, showing off their depictions of a woman, with different positive quotes coming in and out of them to portray what a woman was.

A woman at a desk in the foyer welcomed us, asking if we were new visitors. As we were, we filled an interest form and were told that we were just in time, as "Freedom to Speak," a session for you to be open, had just started. We were guided to the room, that it was conducted in, and as we entered, we got greeted by everyone around the circle. We found some seats to join in the circle and then Coleen began to speak, "Hi everyone it's really good to see our regulars amongst us today as well as new faces," at which point she looked at me and Celine. "Let us begin. Who will be the first to present themselves to the group and introduce herself?"

A lady remains seated and begins to speak, "Hi my name is Laura and I need your help. The group responds back to her introduction. She continues with, "I'd been with my partner for a couple of years and he was the nicest man I could've ever dreamt about meeting. When I did, I couldn't imagine that my dream would ever end. He used to spend any free time he had with me, join in with the family outings with my son and I, smother me with affection and all those things you longed for and never got, he gave. There was one time we went on a break together and it was beautiful, we booked a hotel by the beach with the windows facing outward to it. One night we had the most magnificent sunset, he photographed it, was a memory only we could cherish. The morning after breakfast we walked along the beach happily, a wave came and hit the rocks drenching me. He laughed, whilst I then tried to capture the moment a wave came and did it to him. The weekend was momentous, each of our pasts shared, our future spoken, seemed like this would be the start of something special but I was mistaken. It started to be small things at first snapping at me about minor things (even though I was doing tasks that would benefit him), ignoring my phone calls and saying he was doing something for a family member, so he didn't hear it, lying about incidents that was insignificant. He thought I was stupid, I allowed him to continue to play me, as he drained more energy from me. I started to not recognise myself and my actions, but it's not until people started to tell me that there was something not right with this guy, I began to see the cracks. He was sick in the head, taking me for some dickhead, saying one thing to me and another thing to the other woman whilst we were both believing we were the only one. He started to drift away, when he could tell I was no longer appealing, after he'd taken all he could, and I had nothing left literally. I gave my all, my heart, to eventually be alone with my hopes, my dreams I had for us. We were supposed to be building an us, now what have I got now? I feel disheartened, unconfident and empty. How did I allow someone to strip all the goodness from me, when all I did was bear my soul to him, believing he felt the same way?

Coleen steps in, "The reason is, it's in a woman's nature to come in and compliment the man, add value to what we believe he has to be the King he should be. We are the Queen, we lead, we have a mission to create the vision. He had a hidden agenda, you trusted his intentions, but he demanded way too much than he was offering. We often have takers, he was a taker not giving anything substantial to the table except baggage he had collected off his own self-doubt, lack of security, confidence and worth. He didn't have the preparation instilled in him to be the man you adored. It wasn't your fault Laura, and that's why we're here to restore what was taken from you and bring you back to form. Thanks for sharing Laura.

Another lady puts up her hand, Coleen asks her, "What is your name?"

She responds, "My name is Emma."

"Hi Emma, what brings you to our group today?"

"I don't know where to start"

"Start anywhere you'd like, this is your space, to be free to speak anything in confidence."

"Okay," she says as she begins. I met this guy we had no interest in the slightest in each other at first. I was friends with his friend, so we saw each other around at the same events and didn't think anything of it. I then started having my eye on him, his persona, energy for performing intrigued me so I let myself talk to him and get to know him. It took a while for him to want to get to know me, but we began meeting each other for rendezvouses and that became our thing. When an event finished in the early hours, it'd be habit for him to come to mine or me go to his. He then got a girlfriend and we still allowed ourselves to see each other, the sex was good and there were no official feelings between us, it was just for fun.

Then after a few years had passed, everything changed we actually really liked being in each other's company and were besotted. I found out I was pregnant, it was a shock as we'd always been so careful. This is when I saw the real side of him as he was displeased with my news. He said he loved his girlfriend, he didn't love me, and that this was going to ruin his life. He even mentioned that if I continued with the pregnancy, he would kill himself as this is how much it'd destroy him. He then changed his tune to say that he'd spend more time with me, we'd do more things together, just don't go through with the pregnancy. After weeks of battling on my decision and changing my appointment twice, I went through with a termination. I made this choice, as I was thinking about him and how it'd affect him, and I didn't want him to do something stupid on a decision I made, for a seed that was not actually even formed. The thing is, the termination didn't work, as I did not shed any blood. I thought this was a sign that my baby was still alive, and I would have to come to terms with becoming a mum, even if it would change my life dramatically. I made up my mind, I was going to do this, as I only made this decision as I thought things between us may work. It was the worst decision I'd made as when I went to the clinic, they told me I had to go through in having the surgical procedure instead of the two pills that I had previously took, as the medical team informed me there would be definite birth defects if I continued with the pregnancy. I was heartbroken. When he knew it was done, he distanced himself from me, he had no reason to stay around anymore. I felt alone and at a loss as I came out with nothing from the time, I had given to him except guilt and pain. What do I do now to cope with what I allowed myself to go through?

"Does anyone want to give Emma an answer of what they'd do?" says Coleen looking around the room.

Celine puts up her hand and talks, "Accept the decision you made at the time was the right choice and you needed to do it. It may feel crap that you feel you have nothing to show for it, but least you can build on having a future with someone else that is for you and who will be honest about what you two are. It's hard to think he's getting on with his life, but you can't change his emotions only yours. At some point he'll realise, but by that point it'll be too late."

"That was a good start Celine, thank you. Emma, first and foremost, it is talking about how you're feeling and not bottling it up. Trying to keep it bottled up is going to do more damage than good. Seek professional help like counselling, so you are talking about your thoughts to someone who knows how to master these situations and guide you on the right options. Overall, keep talking, set goals and enjoy the time you have as a single woman to find yourself. Once a child comes, they'll be occupying most of your time, so anything you may want to do for yourself, will go on the back-burner as the child will have to take precedence."

Emma says thank you and we continue to listen to others who wanted to share. 'Freedom to Speak,' share time lasted for a good hour and half and we ended the session with the Yana plea.

I take back the power that was stolen from me, by the empowerment of my strength I gain from shared experiences of mine and others. The old me is gone I cut all ties of the old me. That is not me. I want to bring forth the me, that wants to represent who I am as a woman, that though I may have had traumas in my life, I won't let that define who I am. I am going to arise and inspire to be myself, live my dreams and grow through struggles, truly inspired to wear the invisible badges of strength, confidence, courage, compassion, and fearlessness.

After that we ended with light conversation and refreshments and opportunity to mingle with other members and share any feedback to Coleen and enquire about other services Yana provided.

MONEY TO BE MADE

Whe got back, before Celine and I can get comfortable, my phone rings.

RING RING… RING RING… RING RING… RING RING…

"Hello this is Daphne; how can I be of service to you?"

"Yes, it is, and what is your name?... Campbell. Okay... So, you will need me to bring another lady with me?... Okay, that may be possible," as I look over to Celine. Well as we usually work alone that will be £150 each for the hour for you and your friend. Are you happy for me to continue? Okay, good. Have you got any preferences in what you would like us to wear, not to wear, as some men don't like women showing any flesh?... Hahahahahahaha, of course. So, have you used this kind of service before?... So, I don't need to alliterate for you the obvious details then?... I don't want to come across patronising... Of course, sir... Have you got anywhere in mind, you want to go?... Let us know the meeting place once you've spoke to your friend, and I'll send you a confirmation text for later on... I look forward to meeting you Campbell... Likewise, goodbye."

I put the phone down and look at Celine, eyes beaming at her, "So are you going to thank me then?"

"For what?"

"I've got a job for us tonight £150 for an hour, me, you, this guy Campbell and his friend."

"Doing what?"

"Well what would you usually do if you were to go on a date? Dress up, be friendly, have a good time."

"Yeah I could maybe do that, if I knew what they looked like."

"Don't worry about that. Let's get ready and hope for the best. I've had some not so pretty guys in my time doing this, and they've been flattered that they were even able to get that close in conversation with me."

"Okay," Celine responds unenthusiastically.

"I want to hear a little more life in it Celine."

"Okay Caroline, thank you I'm so excited to do this job with you, it's going to change my life," Celine says sarcastically.

"That was rather sarcastic, but I'll take it as though you're ecstatic."

"So, what did he say he wanted us to wear or not to wear?"

"He didn't seem too bothered, he just said what we feel comfortable in."

"Well that's a little basic."

"Yeah, I know. I didn't get much off him on the phone, he seemed like he knew the drill."

"Did he say where he got your number from?"

"Yes, someone from this bar I'd been to, gave it to him, or something like that."

"You didn't think to ask for more details?"

"No, I don't have my business cards just lying around anywhere and it's my only form of advertising, so it would have to of been given in some way, unless someone had, had their wallet stolen or something which is a pretty farfetched way to get my card."

"I hear you there. So, what am I looking for exactly to wear?" Celine says as she walks towards my closet.

"You have so many clothes I don't even know what and how to choose."

"I'll make a suggestion for you... A little black dress portrays simple, sophisticated, confident and not trying too hard"

"Okay great I'll just sift through these ten black dresses."

Caroline laughs, "My wardrobe isn't that bad."

"It's not, but you seriously don't need anymore. I know I don't get to buy much for me because of the kids, but I know you've probably not even wore half of these."

"Hmmmm, yep you're right, so remove whatever takes your fancy."

"Really?"

"Yeah, least I know they'll be appreciated more."

"Thanks Caroline, you've been so accommodating."

"It's no problem, I've never had a sister I could share clothes with and I've always wanted one, so you might as well fit the title."

"Thanks, not sure if I should take it as a compliment, but alright."

"Take it any way you like. I've not had anyone I can be close to like this for a long while, so I guess I should thank you for your company too."

"Hey, don't get soppy on me now."

"Pfff, that's as far as it goes... Anyway, let me check my phone, see if I've been sent the details of where we're heading."

I go and check my phone.

"Okay so we're going to meet at the rented apartments on Grange Road. We've got a few hours now to spruce ourselves up and have one drink to calm our nerves."

"Do you usually have a drink?"

"Yeah, especially if it's someone I haven't met before. I like to not show I'm nervous as I know they'll be, if they've not done something like this before."

"So, what happens when we get there?"

"Well as we're going together, which I've not done before, it'll be very similar. We will meet them at the apartments, and from there we will head to a bar."

"So, you're not sure if they've got an apartment and want us to chill with them there?"

"Well if that is the case, we will have a drink there, and leave if we're not happy. They will be paying for an hour service of our presence, as long as we're chatting and they're enjoying our company, it'll be fine. An hour goes fast, so improvise, if anything, show your best trick."

"I don't have one."

"I don't know... Ask him to play- 'I have never'."

"Caroline, you're not giving me much confidence here."

"That's why I said, if anything improvise. Be yourself and you can't go wrong."

We start to get ready, do our makeup, whilst having a white wine spritzer, listening to some music in the background.

"Lil bitch, you can't f@%* with me if you wanted to, these expensive..."

Celine laughs, "You're starting to get a feel of my kind of tunes then Caroline?"

"Getting there, slowly. You ready?"

"Yes, just need to choose some shoes."

"What about these?"

"Ooooooo red bottoms. What!! These are bloody shoes."

"Hurry up girl, stop playing and let's get going, you keep them lyrics for when we get there."

We grab our bags and head to the car and put the address in my sat nav. We sing along all the way to some songs Celine had put on as a mix on my player, they made the journey that more quicker. As we reach our destination and I'd pulled the handbrake up and put into neutral, I turn to Celine, "We're here, let me give him a call."

RING RING... RING RING

"Hi Campbell, we're here, where are you?... Okay, then we'll buzz up."

I park up on the side street and head to the front of the apartments.

"So, we're going to have a drink and then head to the bar?" Celine asks me as we approach the door.

"Yes," nodding back.

"It's Daphne buzz us up," I say to the intercom.

Beeeeeeeeeeeep Beeeeeeeeeeeep

We get in the building and walk to the lifts to make our way to the designated floor. We get to the door and a Jamaican Indian man opens the door. He is in his early 50s I'd guess, rough but smart casually dressed. He obviously isn't my type but will have to roll with it and make this the quickest hour of my life.

"Hi, I'm Daphne, nice to meet you," stretching out my hand.

"Nice to meet you," Campbell replies.

"Hi I'm C..."

"Caprice," I interrupt as I'd forgot to tell Celine to make up her own alias for the job.

"Nice to meet you both," the friend of Campbell called Connor says.

"Likewise," Celine smiling.

We all find a seat, Celine on the sofa with her guy who actually was in his 30s, and I found a seat at the breakfast counter, whilst Campbell opened a bottle and poured us all drinks in the open plan kitchen. Celine and her guy were already getting acquainted, seemed as though they had a liking for each other. I looked at Campbell half smiling, in my head I'm saying, let this hour end as quick as possible.

As he passes me my drink, he wastes no time to ask me,

"Are you going to accompany me into the other room, so we can give them some space to talk?"

"Yeah sure, okay then."

Before I leave the room, I stop and tell Celine I'll be going next door.

"We'll be in the other room if you need me, you going to be okay?"

Celine replies, "I'll be fine don't worry about me."

"Okay then babe," I said.

"You're a protective one," Campbell says.

"Yeah, she's like a sister to me, it's a no questions asked obligation to have each other's back."

In my head I'm thinking, is it too soon for Celine after circumstances with Paul? Is she really ready to be around men at this time? These thoughts didn't occur to me until now. I thought more about having her join the business with me, than what a compromising position I could potentially be putting her in.

I follow him into the bedroom and he asks me to sit with him on the bed.

I sit down, and he says, "You going to show me some love?"

I swiftly move my head back, a bit taken back and reply, "Steady on, let's talk a while, so we can get to know each other first."

"I know what I've paid for and it's not to talk."

"Well I'm letting you know how I do business. To ensure that I have a regular customer base and build a good business relationship, I need to build a rapport with you first."

"I'm telling you as the customer, I don't want all that. I've given you money and I expect you to show me a good time."

"I think we've got our wires crossed, somewhere. I am a professional escort and that's what I expect to maintain. You've called me saying you've been given my contact details but I'm now wondering from where, as my referrals are usually very up to standard. I've never met anyone like you."

"Well I can't help you there, I am who I am and I'm not changing for no one. I'm not here to have a conversation with you, so less talking and more action."

"I'm telling you, I will give you back your money and I will go on my way, as this is not how I conduct business. I do not feel happy or comfortable to be in your company right now."

I get up to go and he grabs my wrist. I try to stay calm and ask him to lose his grip on my arm please. I don't always remember my handles but in this instance, it was a must.

"I'm asking you nicely to sit down," he says.

"I don't want to, I'm going."

As I refuse to do what he says he drags me back so I'm sitting back on the bed, his hand remains on my wrist.

"I don't know what your problem is, you know what your job is but you're trying to resist, like this is some PG movie. You're a hoe, don't need to be all innocent with me, I don't care for nothing but what you're giving me."

I look at him and I'm starting to get angry, "A hoe? No, I'm a professional worker. I don't need your money, I can go elsewhere with someone who respects the job."

"Don't make me laugh, you expect a guy to respect you when you obviously don't respect yourself."

He now has his other hand on my other wrist and he leans his body towards me, until he's pushing himself onto me. He starts to get his face by my chest nuzzling at my breasts to try get them out. I ask him to stop without being too loud as I don't want to alert Celine as yet, as I need to try and defend myself.

"Would you stop? I want you to get off me."

"These taste too good baby girl," as he's nibbling on my chest.

"I don't like it, you need to get off me now!"

He has now got himself sitting on top of me, me under him, with him holding both of my wrists. He's kissing my neck and chest and putting his mouth wherever he wants it to go. I feel paralysed, even though his body is so heavy on top of me, I know he's too strong for me to try and struggle. I'd never been compromised in this position before, so I don't know what to do. As he let's go of one of my wrists, I can judge he's putting his hand down his boxers to get his dick, I'm unsure what he's going to do with it. He starts to wank himself and grabs my hand, so I can do it for him as he makes noises to himself sliding up and down my body whilst kissing my lips. I feel physically sick, I don't know what to do but lay there and let him do what he wants to do for now, as long as he does not try to put his dick anywhere else. I don't know how long I was wanking him for, but he takes his dick from me and starts to rub it along my leg, I can feel him starting to rub it closer and closer towards my middle and I scream out noooooo. He shouts back, "SHUT UP BITCH!! TAKE IT!!"

As I start to wriggle my body, to prevent it. I continue to call out now, not caring to be heard, HELP!!!HELP!!! as I feel his dick is now inside of me. He gives out a groan of yeesss, that feels good. I have tears coming down my eyes as I can't do anything but allow him to control my body. "SOMEONE HELP ME PLEASE!!!"

"Get off me," I cry. "Leave me alone, you're hurting me, I don't want this."

He says, "It doesn't feel like it, it feels like you're enjoying it, you're wet. We didn't need to go this route, you could have just said you'd make me happy and be done with it, now you're making me look like the bad guy."

As he continues to thrust and I'm crying my eyes out, Celine bursts into the room.

"GET OFF HER!!" as she pushes him as hard as she can off me. She manages to get him off me, but as he gets up, he swings his arm back and gives Celine one back hand at the side of her face which sends her falling to the ground.

"That was rude of you, don't interrupt me like that again. You've got my friend next door, are you jealous? I saw you staring at me when you came?" As he draws his attention to Celine, on the floor.

"You can have me too, after I'm finished with your friend."

As she does not respond, he then starts to head back towards me again. I'm huddled on the bed crying, holding unto myself, "Don't please."

He says, "Where was we?"

Before he could move any closer to me, out of nowhere, Celine gets up, comes over and hits him over the head with the lamp-stand. She does it repeatedly, over and over again.

"STOP CELINE!!STOP!!" I beg her. "You're going to kill him!"

As she begins to realise what's she's doing, it's too late. He's slumped on the bed, motionless.

"He's dead isn't he Celine? He's dead!" I scream.

Celine is just watching him, with the lamp-stand still in her hand.

Connor comes in very delayed, Celine had said he popped out, "What the f@%* has happened? Nah, nah, I can't have any part of this. I wasn't here. You didn't see me," and he runs out the door.

I look at Celine, "Celine it's alright, it was self defence."

Celine remains in shock staring at Campbell.

"Celine, I'm going to call for an ambulance, okay?"

I still get no response. As I sliver myself to my bag to reach my phone, I get it and call 999, "Can I get an ambulance please?... I've just been raped, and my accuser is on the floor, I'm not sure if he's dead."

I hang up the phone and I take myself to Celine. I take the lamp-stand from her hand and drop it on the floor and hug her. "Everything's going to be okay, I've got you," as she cries in my arms.

"Thank you, Celine, for protecting me. I don't know how I can repay you. I'm really sorry for putting you in this predicament, I'm really sorry."

Connor must have left the apartment door ajar as the ambulance services and the police arrive, making their own way into the room. The ambulance service tends to Campbell first and confirm him dead on the scene. He is put on a stretcher and zipped up into a body bag. The ambulance services ask if we have any injuries, as the accusation of rape had been made. Celine and I are then transported to the police station for forensics and statements. We are at the police station for some time, unable to put an exact time as there were so many evaluations to be done. I had to be stripped, pictures taken of my body, swabs taken for testing, breathalysed for alcoholic intake and blood samples. When it was all complete the police said I was able to go. I did not see Celine throughout this time, I asked them, and they said she would be unable to leave as she would be charged for the murder of Campbell. I said, "No, no, she didn't mean to kill him, she did it in self defence. You can't do this."

They told me that they'd be a court case, so in this time I would have to wait till then. I couldn't believe this was happening, one action caused a spiral of events so quickly. I called my Mum at the police station to pick me up as my car was still left outside the apartments. When she came, I gave her a big hug, and said I just want to go home. It was in the early hours of the morning when we'd returned home, so I didn't talk to my Mum about what had happened and went straight to my room to the bathroom. I put on the shower and climbed out the clothes that the police had given me as they had kept my clothing. I walked into the shower and sat there whilst the water spurted on me. I felt so dirty, I started scrubbing myself violently. I wanted every ounce of Campbell off me, his touch, his smell. When I came out of the shower, I dried myself and put my dressing gown. I threw back some sleeping pills with a glass of water and cried myself to sleep.... eventually.

The morning came, and I was straight on the phone to criminal solicitors to find the best one for Celine, that was the least I could do. I found the best one I could and told them that all invoices should be sent to me. I directed them to the police station she was in and waited for them to give me details of when the court day was. When the lawyer finally got to me, they informed me that the case could go either way for jail time or not, for many reasons they'd need to take into account provocation, intoxication and imperfect self defence.

This worried me as this was the last thing Celine needed; she'd been abused, her child had been abused, she'd just had her kids taken away from her, she was trying to get her life back on track and then she met me. I only wanted to help her and look where it got me. I should have taken into account her mental state and how she may have reacted in the worst case scenario when we were in a confined environment. There was nothing I could do now, so needed to put behind me the should of, would of, could of, and move forward positively on how we could hope for the best in helping her rehabilitation once she had all charges dropped and could be freed.

ORDER IN THE COURT

The day came for Celine's court date, my Mother Pat came with me for moral support. I really appreciated it as I felt so alone. I had so many feelings about the situation with Celine, that I had neglected the fact it was because Campbell raped me, and he had violated me as a woman and my right to say no to his advances.

I could see Celine in the protected glass, standing handcuffed, she looked withdrawn and pale in colour. She was obviously not coping well in there. When I was able to get her attention, I blew her over a kiss and gestured with my index finger pointing to myself, to my hands on my heart and then pointing my index finger back to her, to show I loved her. It hurt me that she was there, it was all my fault.

I looked around the courtroom to see who had come, there were quite a few members of the public, Coleen had also made attendance for support, and a woman who was sobbing into a tissue with her head down. I wondered who may it could be; a potential girlfriend/ wife of Campbell's? As I stared at her for a while, it came to my realisation, this could actually be Celine's mother, there were similarities in the cheekbones and eyes.

The lawyer Celine had been given, had said that her mother had the right to know what had happened with Celine, as she was still her next of kin. It was amazing how she could turn up a few events too late. Where was she when Celine really needed her the most as a child?

The bailiff said, "Silence. All rise," as the Judge enters the courtroom to his seat at the bench, and then we all sat.

The clerk then called on the case, facing Celine saying, "Number 261 Celine Packman."

Celine then stood to hear what she was accused of.

"Celine Packman you are charged with that of the 18th day of June 2017 you murdered the now deceased Mr. Campbell Jackson pursuant to the section of the Criminal Justice Act 2003. How do you plead, guilty or not guilty?"

Celine pleaded not guilty.

The police prosecutor then stood and outlined the particulars of the offence, at which point I zoned out briefly, to not have to relive the details of that night. I needed to testify, but at this point I rather of not hear the chilling horrific events of that fatal night until then. The police mentioned that upon questioning, Celine, was cooperative with them in giving the full history of events.

Once the police prosecutor had finished his statement, Celine's defence lawyer stood before the court addressing the Judge in response to provide additional information that may assist in making a decision, and if any penalty would be made.

"The accused is a good mother, student and employee who has had no previous record of violence, but only reports of good behaviour, which we have evidence; from lecturers at University as well as the bar she works at. These are unusual circumstances, she would otherwise have not been involved in, but recent happenings include her being the subject of domestic abuse in which she was put in hospital resulting in her children being unable to be in her care. She has also been subject of child abuse from the age of 5 to which has transfixed her opinion of the man being a predator and a danger to her. She has genuine remorse for the crime and is adamant that this will not happen again.

We hear Celine being questioned and the case takes a break. When the case recommences, I give my witness statement, but unfortunately the overall verdict from the Judge is that Celine is guilty of voluntary manslaughter, including imperfect self defence. She may have not been found guilty, but the Prosecutor revealed that she had a substantial amount of alcohol in her body. If she were sober, one hit would've been sufficient enough for us to get away. In addition, a call to the Police before entering the room I was in, with the perpetrator, a death could have been avoided.

Celine was sentenced to three years imprisonment and was immediately taken back to prison.

I was heartbroken, I couldn't believe it. I looked around and my mother and the lady I assumed was Celine's mother was no longer in the court room. I made my way out and saw Coleen with Cynthia, (I wasn't familiar with at this time), but she mentioned she worked at the same bar as Celine on different shifts. They both said they were sorry about the result and if there was any support I needed, don't be afraid to ask. I replied thank you for attending and that I may see them soon. As they started to walk away from me, I spotted my Mother talking to the person I thought was Celine's Mother, so I walked towards them. When they both glanced and saw me, the woman I thought was Celine's Mother touched my Mother's arm and walked off.

"Was that Celine's Mother you were talking to?" I asked.

"Yes," my Mother replied.

"What did you both need to talk about? You don't know her!"

"I'll talk to you when you get home. What's important is how are you feeling?" diverting the conversation about me.

"I'm not feeling great at all. I feel it's all my fault, she did something to help me and now she's paying the price. She didn't even want to be there."

"Caroline dear, you can't blame yourself. We all have choices and have to be accountable for our actions. It is sad, as she was trying to protect you, but she had a lot of built in anger from her previous abusers that made her lose control of the situation and neglect her responsibility to not cause detrimental harm until you told her to stop."

"I know you're trying to help mum, but it still does not hide the fact I put her in the situation, she was never used to, and it wasn't her who was in any harm."

"Okay Caroline, let's make our way home and continue talking there."

On our way home the car was quiet, neither me or mum spoke. I guess it had been a long morning of reflection for both us. As we parked up and made our way into the house, mum asked me to come into the study with her as she wanted to talk to me.

I followed her in, sat down and said, "I'm listening, what is it?"

She began to speak, "It was hard living in the household of a father who had an active role in the public eye. You had to be mindful of every action, every conversation, your behaviour, all needed to be on top form entirely.

When we were at home, we could just about be ourselves. We hosted dinners where we would all have to be dressed appropriately, our manners had to be impeccable by addressing guests with their proper title, using the correct cutlery depending on the dish served. We were being watched, and any wrong behaviour would be scrutinised. My life was not my own.

I agree that there should be some form of discipline for children growing up, but mine felt like torture. I couldn't express myself as an individual and there was no choice in various activities, I took part in, just in case it didn't replicate a true representation of the family.

When I was at school I got into mischief as that was the only time, I had freedom. I became part of a group of girls and boys who hung around the back of the playing fields in the woods, part of the cross-country route. This was our hidden social place where we could drink, smoke and have a laugh and be ourselves. The other members of the group's parents were also friends of my father's, so we all had an understanding of what each other were going through.

As I left school, things started to become harder as there was more pressure on me to do well. I had ended up in the Championships for Gymnastics, so training was pumped up to an extra three sessions from two, not including the tuition I had for studies, horse riding and piano.

One day whilst training I really over did it doing the same motion repeatedly, to perfect my triple and a half layout with 1260-degree twist. I over rotated and missed the beam on landing resulting in an anterior cruciate ligament injury, which I had to get a MRI to confirm. The injury I had sustained meant unless I was willing to have the full treatment to make a complete recovery, I would be unable to participate in the Championships and get the top marks I needed. I decided to recover, which gave me extra time on my hands to do things like socialising with friends and venturing to new places.

One night I met someone I became friendly with at a bar who said, "Try this," and I ending up taking it. It was only cocaine. When my parents thought I was sleeping I would sneak downstairs and observe my parents and their pals snort in the drawing room many times, so I didn't think it would become a problem. I got so involved in it, I didn't even care, I just wanted more. It allowed me to come out of myself, which then initiated the whispers of, "Go to Georgie for a quickie." Wherever the night took me, you'd find me in the restrooms with a guy for a quick fling, I shamefully must say, for some of the white stuff.

This is when I met your dad. If I wanted some cocaine anytime, I'd call him, you could say he was my drug dealer. We'd have a quick bang, he got what he wanted and so did I. As my parents, your Grandparents had taken my allowance, (not condoning my wayward behaviour to blow their hard-earned cash), my only option to get drugs quick was to go to your Dad.

It was not long before I ended up falling pregnant with you and I didn't know what the hell to do, as me and your dad was not in the slightest serious about each other. I told your Gran first and she was not impressed but said she'd stand by me and nine months later I gave birth to, two baby girls.

"You what?! Two??" I interrupted.

"Yes!"

"So, did she die?"

"No, she didn't. As your Grandparents did not want to get any slack from their only daughter: one, having a child out of wedlock but two, with a black man. It was just not open for discussion. I wanted to keep you both, so you could both grow up together, but they weren't having it. There's not a day that goes past, where I don't think about her."

"So, what happened to her?"

"We had her adopted."

"I can't believe this Mum... I can't even call you that. You kept me, but gave away my Sister? We both were produced from a black man! So, what's the difference?"

"You were white as snow and your sister dark as cocoa. We were able to pull off in saying you were maybe part Italian if your skin became olive but not any darker."

"You, Gran, Granddad, make me sick. You thought that you kept up appearances and embarrassment from who knew you, but you were mistakenly wrong. I was bullied the whole time at school by other kids calling me 'secret blackie' so you didn't do much of a great job."

"Why didn't you say anything?"

"I tried, but you said, "sticks and stones, ignore them, they're only kids." I was a kid too and those words did hurt as I didn't know who I was."

"I am so sorry Caroline, but I haven't finished what I'm trying to get at and I'm finding it hard, as it is."

"What else is there to say? What can anything you say undo what you've done?"

"As you know in court, I spoke to Celine's Mother."

"What has she got to do with anything?"

"Let me finish Caroline! As I was saying, she's telling me she's come to support her Daughter as a last attempt to show her she's sorry for everything she's allowed happen to her and that she's here now to reconcile. She reveals the greatest regret and the reason she walked out of court, was Celine not knowing who her real father was. The man, the deceased, who she was sentenced for manslaughter, was in fact Celine's biological father."

I'm now gawking at my Mother confused and in shock. There's complete silence, so I break it, "... Celine's Father raped me? Celine killed her Father not knowing he was her Father? I have a twin who I don't know is even alive?"

"I know this is a shock to you Caroline but let me continue, so when I hear Celine's Mother's revelation, without any hesitation I respond to her, with the reason why I left the court room too."

"I couldn't care less, I don't want to hear anymore. This is too much!" tears streaming uncontrollably from my eyes.

"Caroline, please, I need to tell you."

"You've told me enough, I don't want to know anymore!"

I'm now standing up, pacing up and down, shaking my head, putting my hands in my hair. I'm beside myself.

"WWWHHHHHY??????WWWHHHHHY?????? When I thought things couldn't get any worse... My whole life has been a lie? What am I supposed to do now? Tell Celine she killed her Father? Go and find my twin? Oh no I can't do that, she got adopted, she has a different name to me? She's black! So where do I start? I HATE YOU RIGHT NOW!!! HOW COULD YOU DO THIS TO ME!!!"

"I'm sorry, I'm really sorry. I didn't want it to be this way, believe me, please Caroline, I love you."

"You don't love me. You don't know the meaning of the word. My twin is part of me, but you didn't love her enough to keep her."

As I said it, my Mother slapped me in the face, it stung as I put my hand on my cheek.

"HOW DARE YOU? YOU DON'T KNOW HOW IT WAS FOR ME! HOW HARD IT WAS? I'VE MADE SURE I'VE GIVEN YOU EVERYTHING YOU NEEDED!!!

"YEAH, EVERYTHING OTHER THAN A FATHER!!!"

"YOUR FATHER RAPED YOU!!!"

"WHAT???"

"It shouldn't have come out like that," as she starts to walk towards me with her arms out.

"What did you say? Say it again?" I'm standing motionless. "I feel like... I feel... I feel..." Then from the pit of my stomach, up my throat and out my mouth, I was sick. I didn't feel sick, I was physically sick from the thought of what happened that night. I couldn't even bare to say it, as then it would mean it was real.

As I sit down to try console myself and wipe my mouth, I look at my Mother. "Well done to the both of you, the mother of the year awards go to... neither of you! You and Celine's mum kept us away from knowing who our father was, we incidentally bump into each other, get to know each other, one of us gets raped by him, the other kills him and ends up in prison."

"It wasn't like that Caroline. He didn't want me to have you, especially when he found out I was having twins. Celine's Mother told me, he was a one-night stand for her. She tried to look from him when Celine was born, and he didn't want to know either."

"How else am I supposed to take all this? You both were irresponsible and did not have the inclination to think, it's best that I tell my Daughter her Father lives in the same county as her. He may have not wanted to know, but at least when she's at an age she can make her own choices, she can make up her own mind. All you needed to do is give us a name and we could have done what we will with it... We've got social media now mum, wouldn't have been too hard to search on Facebook for him and potentially the rest of my family. If both of you did that, then maybe Celine and I would have known who each of us were and we wouldn't be in the position we are now. Oh my gosh, Celine and I are sisters. I've made my sister go to prison and maybe not even see her kids again. No... Nooo...Noooo...NOOOOOO"

"CAROLINE, calm down!"

"NO! NO! I'm not calming down.

I met Celine in an abortion clinic, brought her out of hospital where she disclosed to me she was in an abusive relationship and it resulted in her losing her children. She was at her wits end. I brought her into our home for her to feel safe and give her warmth and to build a friendship with me, at last I thought I was now connected to someone who understood me and now you tell me she is my bloody sister and neither of us had a friggin clue. I can't cope, all of this is too much.

ALL THIS TIME, ALL THIS TIME, I had a sister, let me rephrase two sister's I could have related with, who I'd have been able to talk to... And it's not until now after all the shit I've been through, raped by the man who's supposed to be my Father, I find out I've got this extended family I knew nothing about... I'm gone! I can't stay here a minute longer in this house with you. I just want to be sick! I can't fathom any of this! I feel like this is a terrible dream and I can't wake up," I burst into tears, my life is a sham!

"Caroline... Wait... Come back!"

She's blubbering and screaming but I don't care. I hate her right now. I run out the house, the tears stinging my eyes and blurring my vision, but I don't care, I just need to get out, unsure of where my mind is right now. I feel like I'm not present in my body, things are happening around me but I'm none the wiser. I don't even know where to go, what to do, should I get drugs? I want Celine, talk to her, give her a hug, tell her I'm here for her. I was grateful before, but even more so, as now I can say my sister saved me, anything could have happened to her, but she didn't care. Maybe everything may have turned out differently for the both of us, when we were younger we could have gone to the same school, plaited each other's hair, did dance shows together, so many things... My twin, what about my twin? Where is she? Is she still alive? How did her life turn out? Does she know about me? I don't know, so many questions spiraling in my mind with no answers. I then think should I go to YANA and see if Coleen is there, as I need someone right now, someone to tell me it'll be okay and they're there for me. Coleen and I could possibly get a visit booked in to give Celine the news.

I decide to jump in my car and head to YANA. When I get there, I start looking for Coleen. I get to the conference room and freedom to speak is in session, and she is in there, so I take a free seat and listen in until the lady finishes speaking.

When the lady finishes speaking, Coleen speaks and says, "Have we got anyone else who wants to share?" I put my hand up uncertain of what will come out but I'm ready.

"Hi ladies, you may recognise me from a few sessions ago, as well as the recent news headline you may be aware of I'm connected to, RAPE LEADS TO MURDER. I am here as I need someone to talk to, anybody who'll listen, to be able to unload all these troubles that are attacking me. I am stuck in a place where I'm unsure which way to turn, and what is next intended for me. I've just come from my family home, leaving my Mother, who I've just found out has been lying to me my entire life. I now know why after recent revelations, I have been fighting my whole life against some kind of force that has prevented me to move forward. I can admit to myself and to you all, as I have nothing else to lose, I am a drug abuser, I am bulimic, I am an escort amongst other things I'm probably not aware of. I have these problems as I have been fighting with my identity. I don't know who I am, I never have. I've been bullied from as far back as I remember, I tried to damage my body to fix it the way I thought would've made others happy, but it didn't. I felt more pain before the action I took damaging myself, than after not receiving the answers I was looking for; with every snort I took, each vomit I brought up and every man I laid down with. I know now, I need help. I need support, I need to know who Caroline is? What does Caroline enjoy doing?

As I was saying before about my Mum lying to me, we came back from the court case after we heard the guilty conviction and she was explaining about how she met my Father. I never knew who my Father was, from his name, to his nationality, down to if he was alive or not. It was never topic of conversation. Although I had tried in the past to bring it up, I'd got shut down by my Mother. The revelation is, that not only do I know who my Father is, he is the supposed victim of the murder plus rape on myself. To top it off, my friend who is in trouble and charged with the offence, is my half-sister. Tell me what do I do with news like that? As I sure don't know.

That was the first time since everything happened, that I'd been able to openly share intimate details in public. It was very difficult but thank you for your patience and being such great listeners."

"We have now completed our session in Hall one, so when we come back you will begin your new session in Hall 2 with Cynthia and Coleen. We know this is a long day, and as we want everyone to be recuperated and be fully charged to continue this afternoon. As promised we've provided lunch in hall 3 ready to reconvene in an hour. If you have time once finishing your lunch, have a look at the worksheets in your pack until we reconvene. Thank you again for your participation so far," says Caroline ending her session on destruction leads to empowerment.

A.W.W CONVENTION WORKSHEETS

REFLECTION

IDENTITY

Who are you? Where do you come from? Culture? What are your interests? Habits? Career? Personality? Emotions? Beliefs? Dreams? Talents? Goals? Make an image below of what defines who you are

PERSONAL IMAGE

Are you happy with your appearance?

What's your best features?	What's your least favourite features?

What could you do, to love them a bit more or embrace them if you can't change them?

……...

……...

....

……...

....

There are various ways we abuse our bodies? What ways do you possibly do this? What are the negatives to these? What could you use as an alternative for these?

……...

……...

....

……...

What are your values? What do you believe in?

What are your best qualities?

……………………………………………………………………………………

……………………………………………………………………………………

……………………………………………………………………………………

……………………………………………………………………………………

……………………………………………………………………………………

……………………………………………………………………………………

……………………………………………………………………………………

Who can you trust? Why do you trust these chosen people? Have they shown you a side of you, you can't trust?

……………………………………………………………………………………

……………………………………………………………………………………

……………………………………………………………………………………

……………………………………………………………………………………

……………………………………………………………………………………

What makes you feel positive even at times you would rather not.

……………………………………………………………………………………

……………………………………………………………………………………

……………………………………………………………………………………

What do you love about yourself?

....

....

....

....

....

What helps you be strong?

....

....

....

....

....

Who do you have that is positive around you?

....

....

....

....

Who do you see as your role model? Why?

. . . .

. . . .

. . . .

. . . .

. . . .

What about you, could inspire others?

. . . .

. . . .

. . . .

. . . .

. . . .

CLICK CLICK

"Welcome back ladies to the last session of the day in Hall 2 about establishing the ultimate purpose of A Woman's Worth with me (Cynthia) and my colleagues Caroline and Coleen. I hope this day has been an eye opener for you; in terms of how circumstances can change your life, how to work through them, the ability to understand the journey and what you need to do to change, to enable your future to be a positive one. To conclude and bring everything together, I will now tell you about my story I promise to keep you engaged."

When you pronounce my name it's not Cin-Tia. I feel like I have to firstly clear that up, for those who think I'm Jamaican. I grew up in Westley, so for those who know where I'm talking about, its Cyn-fe-a darling. I have caramel clear skin, afro, tight curled, neck length hair. The only way to tame it, is with a big teethed comb and soft and free curl activator spray. I am officially the definition of #blackgirlhairproblems. I was born in Kinchester, which is stated on my birth certificate, other than this gropey bit of paper, that was all I was given, by my adoptive white parents.

I now reside in Poseley which is the opposite; free and cosmopolitan, surrounded by various bars and restaurants.

My parenting was very strict, I went to private school for a while, where I learnt three languages, French, Spanish and Japanese. Je connais. French for, 'I know.' Fancy aren't I?

Being a teenager wasn't easy, the rules, peer pressure and trying to understand who I was, influenced my decisions because I just wanted to fit in. In our home we didn't see colour, that's why it was so difficult to come to terms with why my adoptive parents, told me they didn't want me anymore at the age of thirteen. I got transferred from one foster care home to another. I believe I either was too demanding for them in terms of what I wanted, as I was accustomed to getting what I wanted before. I felt like I was living in a prison, with the windows persistently locked and unable to open, even for fresh air.

As I became part of the system at such a young age, that is where I would remain, stuck as a statistic of numerous stereotypes.

If I were to describe myself I'd say I have the ethics of Erykah Badu a split between... Let me stop myself right there, you can get a feel of who I am as we go along.

This would be the introduction of how I'd describe myself in the various forum profiles I was associated with, which helped me to connect with likeminded people such as myself, open up about who I was and practice my writing skills. I am a spoken word artist and what helped me from such a young age was expressing myself through writing with rhyming. I had to do this each time I experienced something traumatic, as I didn't know any other way to let out how I was feeling.

On most evenings I would perform in my workplace.

On a familiar autumn weekday evening, in a back-street bar in Baringham, UK, you hear the simultaneous clicking of fingers.

Click....Click....In a world full of destruction and pain, I see no light at the end of the tunnel for me to gain.

Click....Click....The colour of my skin deters their eyes, but what really lies within mine?

Click....Click.... Do I need to iron my hair, bleach my skin?... Or do I embrace my birthright with two feet in.

Click....Click....The governments destroying my ability to be in control, my actions don't feel like me no more.

Click....Click.... Identity's fading, diluting, the mere knowledge I preserve, unable to sustain, it truly hurts.

Click....Click.... What do I do? What can I say? Do I do what Dr. Luther the King and Mandela conveyed, stand up for truth and you will prevail?

Click....Click.... I, I, I, no I in we but in oui. Yes, we. We need to unite, we need to ignite the flame of empowerment, strength and pride. Click....Click.... Of the unfinished works our ancestors left for us to defeat.

There's a faster pace clicking, click, click, echoing throughout the tea light lit bar,

As I say thank you and walk off the stage, someone grabs my attention, "You were great," said a dark chocolate skinned man with tidy dread hair, and the most beautiful smile. It was clear to see that he was well groomed with his straight white teeth, oil polished skin and the aroma I will assume was a Tom Ford scent. He wore this tight short khaki sleeved shirt that was not fully buttoned and exposed his perfectly ripped chest. Hmmmmm.... I was in heaven.

"Oh, thank you. Are you a regular to these weekly sessions?" I replied.

"I've been here a few times, but not heard any of your spoken word or seen you before, if I'm being totally honest," he said.

"I've not long come back from a spiritual retreat. I travelled from Thailand and ended my trip in the Himalayas."

"Okay, is that your thing then? Spiritual journeys, meditation, synchronising with the universe etc.?"

"Yes all of the above and more."

"So how did you come by this path....?"

He places his hand on the front of his head, "Where are my manners, would you like a drink?"

I smiled, "Yes, that'll be nice, Hennessey, neat please."

"Wow... lady knows how to drink."

"Well if you going to drink, might as well choose one, that'll do what's it's intended to do first time."

The bar worker gives us our drink, we tap our glasses towards each other and take a sip.

I put my glass down and ask, "What is your name?"

"Oh, we haven't fully introduced ourselves. My names Malcolm," he said with his hand out to shake mine.

"Cynthia, it's nice to meet you," gently shaking his hand.

"So, what's your plans now then beautiful?"

"You tell me," Malcolm asked.

"Well you can always come back to mine."

"Sounds like a plan. What you waiting for? Come on."

So, this was common procedure, drop some lyrics at the bar and hope that a sexy guy would hear so I was sorted in the bedroom department for the night.

At the bar is where I met most guys, convenience I guess, and I knew what kind of guy would come in on particular nights, so it made it easier in looking, and sieve out the undesirable ones.

I hadn't been looking for anyone as a permanent fixture, fun came first, especially once I knew that my coochie could only be used for one thing now, since I was unable to conceive. I was nineteen when I officially found out I couldn't. I had to have a hysterectomy. At the time I had no interest in having kids, so it didn't bother me and after my own experiences whilst I was young, I wanted to try have a more normal life by myself. I try not to think about it, as it's something I have to live with every day. I'll give you more about the details on what happened, later on.

As I had briefly mentioned I was adopted at the age of thirteen my adoptive parents decided they didn't want me anymore. I remember it like it was yesterday, it was a bit of a kick in the teeth if I'm being honest. You made a decision that you would love me, care for me better than my birth parents could, but when you decided it wasn't exactly how you planned it out to be, you thought, let's give up.

It's not a decision you carry out lightly, so how did you decide to just give up and put me out to join the collective of unwanted teenagers, who you know will find it more difficult to be located in a loving family, as we're not a cute baby, and come with years' worth of baggage that no one really wants to deal with?

I remember that day, it was a half term morning. I got dressed, chilled in my room and wrote in my writing pad. Then my adoptive mum knocked on my bedroom door and said, "Pack your things together."

I said, "Are we going on a last-minute holiday?"

She said, "Bring… what you don't want left behind, if you couldn't come back."

"I don't know what you mean, Mum?"

"Cynthia, please do what I ask, don't make it more difficult than it already is," and then she shut the door behind her.

I was confused, I didn't understand what she meant, but I got my suitcase from under my bed and I started to pack. I put in my favourite clothes, basic toiletries along with my writing pad and pen and once I had finished I waited for her to come back. When she did, she asked me to come downstairs with my bag, as it was time.

What was with all the riddles? Be straight with me I wasn't a child, I was thirteen, I had common sense enough for you to tell me the truth, but they decided against it; they were ultimate cowards. As I reached the bottom of the staircase, there were two people that I had never seen in my life with Mum and Dad. I looked at them, baffled, "So... who are you then? There was a pause. Are you going to answer me?"

After what seemed like a long silence, they said, "We're Social Workers. You're going to come with us now."

I replied, "Why?"

They said, "You're unable to reside here anymore, so you will have to come with us, so we can find you an alternative residence for the time being."

"What!!! Are you kidding me?"

I start shouting, "No no no, don't do this, Mum, Dad, tell them it's a mistake, I can stay, you can change your mind. I'll be better, I'll do anything, just don't make me have to go. No!! No!! No!!" I repeat.

The social workers are urging me to come out the house, as I try to look at my parents for some indication that they'll say something, do something, anything, but they just stand there. I say, "Fine then, if that's what you want, I'll go and I'm not coming back EVER!"

My Mum is crying, and my Dad is trying to look solemn, as he puts his arm around Mum and directs her back into the house, he shuts the door. I go in the back of the car and peer out the back window. I watch the door of my house, the windows, to see if there's any movement, but there isn't. I turn around and gaze out the car window it's starting to rain, inevitable to match this gloomy moment.

We end up at the social services office where I sit in a playroom waiting, whilst they call around to get me a placement for the night and indefinately.

As I wait bored of being bored I take out my writing pad out and write:

They told me they didn't want me.

I didn't belong to them you see.

Our ties weren't entwined by blood or genes.

The links were tarnished from the start.

An imbalance of familiarity like contaminated waters, forcing them to believe that ultimately our cultures would never unify.

Thanks for half raising me, with hope and courage that won't manifest in me, as you were inadequate for the role to prove the stereotypes wrong. Sorry if I might sound ungrateful, let me rephrase, thank you, as I'll now be able to unearth the strength and envision of who I really am.

It was difficult to come to terms with my adoptive parents donating me elsewhere like a present you may gently decline to the back of your closet until someone came around and said, "I'll take it." The part I found hard to get around was not knowing why they just gave up. Least my birth parents did the humane deed and gave up prematurely, so I would be unable to reminisce on happy childhood memories.

Yes, I was a troublesome teenager, but who wasn't, no worse than anyone else. Being carted from foster home to foster home I didn't know if I was coming or going.

The hope I previously mentioned for the future, was not apparent as why would it be, I was now in the system till I was eighteen, so this would be my path until I was competent enough to live independantly.

The foster homes I encountered never felt comfortable and I couldn't settle, it didn't feel as though they were my home, and the people there my family. I could not relate or rely on them. It didn't help as, I was being bullied at school. Coming home was not a haven in which I felt relaxed I didn't feel safe and protected from danger. The bullying at school started after I had to leave my all-girls school and go to a more conventional, main stream teaching school. It may have become easier to fit in in the way that no one would know I was fostered, but the area in which the school was, there was very few if any afro Caribbean children, so I stood out from my peers with my distinctive afro hair. There was one girl called Linda who was the schools so called 'it' girl she was popular, and everyone wanted to be around her as she hosted the best parties, had the latest clothing, gadgets etc. She brought it upon herself one day to pick on me, out of nowhere. She came up to me and said, "Oooo I like your hair."

I politely said, "Thanks" and carried on walking.

She continued to follow me with her entourage and taunt me, "So how did you get your hair like that?"

"I was born this way," answering but carrying on walking.

"Oh really," she sniggered.

"So, you don't want your hair straight like ours, rather than a poodle hair mess?"

I stopped and looked at her, "I actually like my hair the way it is, thank you."

"So, you think your better than us, do you?"

"What gives you that idea, because I say I like the way I am, rather than change myself to be like everyone else."

"Someone thinks she can get lippy with me," she turns to face her crew.

"You hear that guys, she thinks she's better than us. What do we do to people who think they're better than us."

She turns back to face me, "Watch your back, you'll soon find out."

Undeterred from her empty threats I walked away and thought nothing of it and carried on to my next lesson. I didn't see Linda until the end of day which was P.E playing netball. Throughout the lesson, I had, if looks could kill glances, they felt so hot it was like she was trying to pierce into my skin, with Superman heat laser vision. I was even in her team, but it didn't make a difference. She'd bounce the ball off the back of my head and say, "Oops, did that hurt?" After I'd said, "Ouch," she'd say, "I didn't think it would, with the cushion you have on top of your head," and then her and the other group of girls would start to laugh.

When it came to the lesson finishing, I was one of the last people to get changed- I preferred to hit the showers in private. When I came out, I started to get myself ready, Linda and her friends reentered the changing rooms. I ignored their presence as I was not afraid of them. I was bold as a lion and strong as an ox.

As I didn't say anything, Linda spoke up, "So you know when I said you would soon find out, what happens to people who think they're better than us, well the time has come."

Thinking they wanted to fight, "I said bring it, I've wanted to smack you the whole lesson."

She laughs, "You can try but I don't think you'll want to with these," as she pulls out a pair of scissors opening and closing them, so I could hear the snapping noise they made, like a crocodile opening and closing its jaws.

I looked at her and said, "What you looking to do with those? Stab me with them? You'll soon get yourself arrested and I'm sure none of your groupies are going to take the fall for you."

"Who said anything about stab?" Before I knew it she said, "Hold her down and restrain her so she can't get loose."

A few of the girls I'd say about five of them, two taking an arm each, with another two taking a leg each. I was kicking my legs out and struggling with all my might that they seated me on the bench to hold me down. I continued struggling to fight them off. The fifth girl went and got my P.E top and stuffed it in my mouth as I spat in one of the other girl's faces. Then Linda walked up to me and began chopping my hair, SNIP SNIP SNIP SNIP SNIP. I was moving my head from side to side to shake her off, so she spoke, "You need to keep still, or I won't be able to get a straight cut."

When she had finished she ordered the girls to let me go, she looked at me and lifted my head up to admire what she'd done.

"I've done a pretty good job, that looks a lot better now, may just take up hairdressing when I leave school I think. See you tomorrow, hope you like your new look," Linda says as her and the girls cackle and walk off.

I sit there and look down at the puddle of curls on the floor, I begin to cry as I start to sweep it up with my hands. I couldn't even put my hands through my hair to feel the damage, I was too scared for the confirmation it was really gone. There were an array of thoughts going through my head, my hair... My beautiful hair... How could they do this to me? This is what made me... Made me feel beautiful, stand out from the crowd... What do I do now? As I begin to finish getting dressed, putting my tights and shoes on, I luckily have a hood on my coat, so I lift the hood to cover my head and zipping the coat up, so it would not be able to come down. I leave the school gym and try to get back to the foster home as soon as I can. When I get back, as soon as I open the door I go straight to the bathroom and lock the door. I stand staring at the mirror and gradually lift the hood off my head. When it's completely off, I gasp. I can't believe it, it's gone. My eyes fill with tears and I begin to cry, but then it diverts to anger, I'm going to show these girls what for, believe me, they're not getting away with this. I wipe my eyes as someone else in the house is needing the bathroom, so I unlock the door and come out. It was my foster sister, Jen, "Cynthia what's happened to your hair? Why have you cut it?"

"I thought it was time for a change Jen, don't worry yourself."

Jen was only a little younger than me around eleven. She had been there for a few years, but when I came she clung to me as an older sister, when she wanted someone to read her a bedtime story or bake cakes with her. I would never have told her the truth, she was too young to understand why anyone would do that and especially if she had the thought planted in her head that it could possibly happen to her. I made my way to my bedroom and got my scissors out to make the remains of my hair look neater as though it was meant to be that way. Jen like any other eleven-year-old told one of our carer's about my hair. I heard the door knock and they came in.

"Cynthia, Jen has told us that you've cut your hair? As I can see you're still at it. What has happened? You loved your hair. Is there something we should be aware of?"

"No Sonia, everything is fine, I just felt like a change I guess."

"Well in future if you want to do something like this you need to tell us first and at least then we will take you to the hairdressers to get it done. Do you still want to go the hairdressers?" she asks.

"Yes, can do, but will have to be tomorrow. I'll have to rock it like this in the meantime as they will be closing soon."

"Okay, I'll get something sorted for the weekend. I suggest you put them scissors down before you have nothing left."

"Alright will do."

As Sonia closed the door behind her, I thought how I could get my own back on Linda and her friends. I wasn't too keen on telling anyone, as I didn't think I had the support, and I knew they'd probably deny it anyway. To help to bring out my emotions over this traumatic ordeal I took out my writing pad and started to write:

My hair is my image, you see it before you see me.

Black, tight curled like poodle maybe, it'd seem.

I prefer, wool of a sheep, tight in shape like the boldness I carry.

115

So, beware little girls quite contrary, I won't be shook.

It was the next day at school and I was ready with vengeance. As I walked in my form class, to assembly and the school yard, everyone stared at me with whispers. "Look at her hair... She looks like a he/she... Eurgh it looks horrible... I heard it was Linda and her crew... How can she come to school looking like that?"

I heard it all day, but I remained to lift my head up high and refuse for Linda and Co. to think they got the better of me, even though it pained me so much inside.

Then Troy who used to go out with Linda walked past me and said, "Your hair looks nice, really suits you," and gave me a wink and carried on walking with his friends. I smiled, the one positive comment I had. Unbeknown to me, Linda and Co. just watched the contact, and she was not happy. She speed walks up to me and pushes me to the ground.

"You think you're clever do you? Trying to go after my ex after what's happened. Think he'd really go for someone like you? Well he wouldn't, you're not his type, so back off if you know what's good for you!" Linda demanded.

A Teacher comes over and says, "Linda detention! We do not tolerate this kind of behaviour in school."

"But Miss," she says stringing out the iss."

"No, I don't want to hear another word unless you would rather answer to the Headteacher," our Teacher said.

So, Linda strutted off and gave me the eye to ensure me she wasn't done.

The Teacher asked me, "Are you okay? Are you being bullied by Linda?"

"No miss," not wanting to tattletale. I was going to make sure I was going to deal with it myself. It was just me and would always be, so I had to stay tough.

As I walked to next lesson, late at this point, I went around the corner and spotted Troy and his boys heading away from the school towards the field. He turned around and saw me stand and look. He gestured his arm to say come, I was like, me, pointing to myself. He nodded and grinned as I made my way over. We ended up going around the side of the playing field which was not actually school property and then Troy pulled out a spliff, he lit it up took a few puffs and passed it to his friend. He looked at me and asks, "Do you smoke?"

I said, "No."

"Do you want to try?" he replied.

"How will I feel?"

"Relaxed and your mind will feel lighter."

"Okay, I guess no harm in trying."

He passes me the spliff, and I take a puff, I start coughing.

He goes, "That can happen when you take in too much first time. Take your time, enjoy it and then breathe it out slow."

I did, and it felt nice, I took more, and I was enjoying the feeling, forgot I'd missed half my lesson at this point.

Troy came out with, "Linda and her posse giving you trouble?"

"Just a little, but nothing I can't handle, will be ready for them next time."

"She's bad news don't even stoop to her level, she's not worth it."

"Why you two break up?"

"She was a nause. I couldn't take her constant babbling and clinginess."

"I see. I'm not going to go out my way to do something but will definitely be on my guard. I'm not having her pull no silly manoeuvre like this again," as I point to my hair.

"She did that? Nah she took it a step too far. I genuinely thought you'd cut your hair, it was well nice before, but this style suits you too, shows off your pretty face."

"No more smoke for you boy, it's really gone to your head," as his friend takes away the spliff and we both laugh.

"I'm just telling the truth enit," he proclaims.

"Okay, cool thanks for the compliment," I said.

I look at my watch, "Can't go to lesson now, so what am I to do now?"

"Well we usually don't head back until the alarm rings, so we can mix in with the crowd of everyone leaving class.

"I get you, makes sense."

Troy and I from then started to hang around each other more often, we wagged lessons and used the time smoking by the field, walked home and to school together, at different times while Linda and Co. were keeping watch. When I was home one night, one of my so-called foster sisters Emma who I didn't converse with to any extent, came to my bedroom with no permission and shut the door.

"You need to stay away from Troy."

"First of all, why are you in my room? Second of all, who are you to tell me who I can and can't hang around with?"

"Cynthia, do you know how dangerous it is for me to come to tell you this? I know what she's capable of, she used to bully me until I ended up deciding to do what she said and joined her posse."

"Thanks Emma but I'm not allowing her to dictate to me like that."

"Like your hair wasn't enough, don't be stupid."

"Looks like I'm going to have to be."

"It's your funeral," and she walks out my room leaving my door ajar. I kiss my teeth, "Rude!"

I didn't read into what Emma said that night, yes Linda had cut my hair but realistically I didn't believe she could do any worse than that.

The morning came, and it was that time Emma was talking about in which, everything had come to a head. I went to school as normal, during the day was the same, didn't hear or see Linda and Co. at all. As it came to the end of the day, I walked home with Troy chatting about usual events that had happened at school, listening to his MP3 player sharing an earphone each. Then out of nowhere I feel someone push me from behind, I trip up but don't fall. I then twist myself around to see who it is, and I feel another push from another direction. I am being pushed from all angles and I'm dazed to the point I can't see clearly; though I am aware it has to be Linda and her crew. They are chanting something or another which becomes louder with screams and words like kick her, kick her, so they all started to kick me all at once, in my stomach, now that I was on the floor, punching me in my head to even pouring some kind of liquid on my head. I'm wondering whilst all this is happening where is Troy? Is he getting beat up? Is he trying to pull them off me with no luck? Or has he scarpered? As I lay there on the ground, the words began to be clearer. "You do it." "No, you do it." "It wasn't my idea." "I'll do it, just like I have to do everything else, she needs to be put down a peg or two once and for all."

As I hear that, I knew it had to be Linda and then I feel another punch in my abdomen once, and then again. I then hear them run off, and Troy's voice comes out of nowhere with a teacher.

"She's been stabbed Miss, we need to call an ambulance," he says.

That was the last thing I hear.

When I wake up, I'm startled by Linda next to my hospital bed. I'm unsure how long I was there for, until I was told later on, that I was unconscious, brought round, and then put in an induced coma due to complications.

"What are you doing here Linda," I try to say through the pain. My painkillers must have been wearing off a bit.

"I'm really sorry Cynthia, I didn't mean to be so horrible to you," she said.

"So why were you?"

"I wanted you to hurt like I was hurting. My parents were splitting up and then Troy broke up with me and when I saw him with you, I was jealous. You were new to the school and you were getting all the attention and I was supposed to be the one that everyone liked. It was wrong of me, and now my thoughtless actions have got me expelled, a criminal record and you may never be able to have kids and it's all my fault because I couldn't control how I was feeling. I know you may not forgive me ever, but I needed to let you know I am truly sorry."

I listened and said I accepted her apology, but she needed to leave.

That was the last time I saw of her, the next time I hear of her name, she'd trespassed on the railway tracks and got struck by a train. I didn't like what she'd put me through, but I wouldn't have wished death on her.

SNOWFLAKE

I'm in my early twenties now, not interested in getting serious with anyone. On my way to work, I make my usual stop off at my favourite coffee shop Beans. I walk to the counter to order a, "One shot caramel cappuccino." I turn my head to look, and a man standing next to me says the same.

"How do you know that's how I like it?"

"You look like a one shot caramel kinda lady"

"Please," I laugh."

"Can you make that two," he says to the waitress.

"Who's the other one for?"

"One for each of us," as the waitress passes him the coffee in take away cups, in which he hands me one.

"I guess here's where I say thank you."

"Well you don't have to, but it'd be appreciated."

"Thank you."

"Have a good day, unless you'd want to share a coffee with me alongside some general chit chat?"

"Maybe next time."

"That's a shame... I see you every morning ordering your one-shot caramel cappuccino and today I get the balls to order it for you and you blow me off," he tries to sigh.

"Really?"

"Yes... Like your hair by the way," as he reaches to try touch a curl.

I dodge my head to the opposite direction of his hand.

"Have you never been told not to touch a black girl's hair?"

"I guess I never got the memo."

"Class yourself as quite the comedian, do you?"

"Well I do like to see if I can put a smile on a beautiful ladies face."

"Aha, definitely a charmer."

I look at my watch and say, "Well since you've already taken up some of my time and my coffee is starting to get cold we might as well sit down and chat."

He scores, "Don't mind if we do. Right this way me lady."

I roll my eyes and follow him to our seats in a quieter area of the shop.

We sit down, and he stares at me whilst I take a sip from my cup.

"So, are you going to talk then?"

"I thought I'd take in this moment," as he continues to gawk at me.

"Okay, so as this seems like you're going to take a while, I'll start. So, what's your name? And where do you come from?" I say.

"Well Cynthia, my name is Mark and I come from Morehampton."

"How you know my name? You been stalking me?"

"Erm, no its on your name badge," as he points it out on my top.

"Oh, yes."

"So where do you live?"

"Up the road, I'm local, live and work in the same vicinity."

"Nice and convenient. I've been commuting down here for the past year because of the regeneration they've been doing around here. I came here once and now it feels like home."

"So, what made you want to talk to me today?"

"Well you may not recognise me but I'm the same guy who says good morning to you as you past the scaffolding around by Ryland Road."

"Oh, that's you. I always kiss my teeth like how you know it's a good morning, wondering at the same time where that voice is coming from."

"Well I thought you may need someone to say it to you, seems like you always have this face on you."

"You mean like my actual face."

"You know what I mean."

I check my watch, "I'll have to go. I need to set up for lunch and bring the chairs and tables outside at work."

"Okay, it was nice to finally get acquainted with you Cynth."

"Please don't do that."

"Not that time yet?"

"My name doesn't need shortening, period. Cynthia is fine."

"So, can I hit you up sometime, I'm heading out tonight if you fancy it?"

I'm thinking to myself, what does this guy want from me, he is clearly not my type, white, bald, dimples but nice physique. This is definitely not a two-way connection, but I've got no plans tonight, so we'll see where exactly he's contemplating.

"Where you looking to go out?"

"Magical down by Lambeth."

"There's a rave on there tonight."

"Yes, that's the one."

"Okay, maybe. Give me your phone."

I type in the numbers and save it. He takes back his phone and puts it to his ear. RING RING RING RING RING

"It's real. Just had to ring it once just in case you tried to give me a faker," he winks at me.

"Don't misuse my number, just text me later what time. Will need to go home beforehand after work to get changed."

"Whatever you say boss."

"Okay catch you later."

I walk off towards work and for some reason I'm smiling to myself. I try to shake it off as I don't know how he was able to keep me in his presence for so long without me biting his head off. His banter was what definately kept me on my toes. I always tried to keep myself away from my opposed culture, since my adoptive parents gave me away, I guess subconsciously I didn't want to get into a predicament that would get me rejected again because of the culture barrier. I may be in for a surprise tonight- looking forward to it.

My day dragged at work, the bar was not very busy, handful of regulars but as I was on an early, it wouldn't pick up until after 5/6pm once everyone had left work for a few drinks with colleagues.

I grab my coat from the staff room and left the bar. The trek home felt tiring, long week on my feet, back and forth to the cellar for crates and changing the barrels. The life of a bar tender was strenuous, let me tell you.

When I got home I had a shower and took a nap, my body needed few winks. The time I woke up I looked at my phone and saw a text from Mark it said, "Hey beautiful, hope you had a good day. Still on for tonight? x"

I text back saying, "Not long woke up, still up for it. What time you heading out?"

Before my phone had chance to go into sleep mode, it pinged again.

"I guess your body needed that sleep to be able to keep up with me all night didn't it lol? 22.30pm alright with you beaut?"

"Yes, that's fine. Want me to meet you outside Magical or you coming to me?" I reply.

"I'll come to you in a taxi, wouldn't want you to be alone on the streets late by yourself x"

"Okay then I'll text you my address."

"See you later ;) x"

I slowly crawl out my bed, and start getting ready, including my makeup. I decide to wear a t-shirt dress which is black with lace trimming along the hem and around the stomach area to separate it as though it was a top and skirt with lace underlining. I wear a lace choker to dress it up with some small heeled Chelsea boots.

As 22.30pm approaches I come out of my flat and he's outside the taxi with the door open waiting for me to climb in.

"Hi," I say smiling.

"Hello. Someone's looking more gorgeous than usual."

"Thank you," as he climbs into the taxi after me.

Driver says where to now? Mark says, "Last stop driver to Magical."

As we are sitting in the taxi with a journey time of approximately 15 minutes, Mark talks a little more about himself. He talks on how he was raised with a silver spoon in his mouth which has permitted him to be anything but humble. The love of his life is his mother who is unwell. He makes sure he pops in to see her at home every other day at least to make sure she is alright, as well as doing her shopping. He is the fourth child of four brothers and two sisters, they're all very close and look after each other. I keep to myself details about me so to not have him trying to pry into my personal life and be guesstimating why I am the way I am.

We arrive at the venue and he comes around to my side of the taxi to open the door for me.

"Thank you," I say to him.

"No problem."

We walk up to the venue and he insists that he will pay. Is he thinking this is a date? As we make our way further inside, first stop is the bar.

"What would you like to drink?"

"I'll have half a cider and black."

He gets a bar tender's attention, "Half a cider and black and a bottle of Corona please."

We get our drinks and take it into another room. We're dancing together, and he is really working it with his dance moves, I'm actually enjoying my time with him. I whisper in his ear, "Do you sniff?"

He looks at me, shakes his head and whispers back, "Your better than that babe."

He takes me by the hand and we find a secluded area of the warehouse to sit down. He says, "I have to be honest with you about my intentions, I like you and want to see where this goes between us. If we're going to move forward in terms of getting to know each other you'll have to come off the white stuff."

"Wow, okay."

"What is it? Did I say the wrong thing?"

"No, I just wasn't expecting you to be so direct. I thought you were just looking for a bit of fun."

"No, not at all. I think you're beautiful and believe your worth more than one night of fun."

As I listened to what he had to say, I remained silent. The majority of men I'd met wanted to just get in my knickers and made it clear, so I didn't think what it actually was I wanted. He actually genuinely seemed to care about my wellbeing and a potential future.

"You okay? Agree with what I'm saying?"

"Yes, yes, sounds good to me."

"Great, shall we go back inside then Cynth?"

I look at him with a discerning look.

"Okay, still not that time?" he chuckled.

"No, I reply."

"Okay," as he moves towards me and kisses me on the forehead.

 The night was surreal, I wasn't used to just buzzing over alcohol alone, but it felt good. We danced, and we danced until the early hours.

"Can I come back to yours then to crash?" Mark asks.

"Yes, but you'll need to take the sofa."

We order an Uber as it'll be the easiest and quickest way at this time, the birds are singing, it's light out and I'm feeling mash up.

As we get back to mine both stumbling through the door, we laugh.

"You enjoy your night?" he says.

"I'm pleasantly surprised that I actually did," I said.

"Really? You thought it'd be a bad night?"

"Well I don't know you and to be completely honest, I haven't fancied a white guy since I was at school, so I guess I assumed all these assumptions in my head before even getting to know you."

"I see, so you fancy me?"

"Maybe."

"Well you didn't say no, so I take it as a positive."

"Hmmmmmm."

"Hmmmmmm, right back at you. So where do you want me to sleep?"

"I did say the sofa."

"If I join you for warmth, I'll promise to be on my best behaviour," he says.

"Okay, you can sleep in my bed, but I'll choose what side you can sleep."

"No problem boss, just no funny business, spooning is as far as it goes, just in case you had any funny ideas."

"Omg, don't flatter yourself. I told you sofa remember?"

He kisses me on the forehead and says, "Thanks for a great night, sweet dreams beautiful."

As he lays his head on the pillow and so do I, we spoon. It actually felt nice. I had so many reservations, but I actually thought I could actually grow to like him.

He's the snow to my flake, like an ice cream. It has a nice ring to it. He wasn't the kinda guy I was expecting, but now I've met him he'll be the only one I'll be pursuing, he's the snow and I'm the flake, when we're together we're snowflake.

COME WITH ME

It started like any other day. Today I'd be boosting my social following and get myself known by busking in town. I set myself up with my portable sound speaker and mic and started with my spoken word usual flow,

"Check, check, you over there. Can you see me? Can you hear me? Do you feel my flow?"

There were a few tents set up opposite me, with tables and flyers. I couldn't see exactly what was happening, but it looked busy outside.

A lady walked over from one of the tents, to my direction and dropped a few coins in my hat and said, "I like your flow."

I said thanks and asked, "What's happening over there?" pointing to the tents.

She responded back, "We're trying to raise awareness, for ladies to get themselves regularly tested, to promote safer sex, amongst other services."

"Would you be interested in taking a test or finding out what we do?"

"Well, since you caught me on one of my good days, I guess I could."

"Okay come with me," the lady replied.

As we reached the tent that was only a couple of meters away, I was asked to firstly fill in my details and tick the boxes of what services would be of interest to me.

"You do quite a bit," I said skimming through all the services.

"Yes, and they're all women based. We don't conduct the tests here. I walk the ladies to the clinic where they're taking place. I can take you there if you'd like, as I've got some forms to drop off there too."

"Yes, then you can tell me more about what you do, I'm all about female empowerment, would love to get involved."

"Really. Well if you were definately interested, it'd be on a voluntary basis at first to be able to determine your commitment to the role."

"I understand, sounds good to me."

"What's your name?" the lady asked me.

"Cynthia," I responded. "Nice to meet you Cynthia, my name is Coleen," shaking my hand.

As we walk up towards the clinic, Coleen shares with me how her organisation Y.A.N.A (You Are Not Alone) started and how she wanted to raise more awareness, so more women were aware of the support network out there for them. She was really inspiring and intelligent, you could tell she was well informed with the topics she was talking about.

We got to the clinic and there were signposts to the area that Coleen was connected with that day. We were welcomed by a male nurse who was Nigerian and very well spoken. Coleen asked, "Where are the women nurses conducting the tests today?"

"We do have one, but she is on her break. I am the other nurse assisting, with a woman student who will be observing them. Do you feel comfortable with me doing it?"

"No. There are a lot of vulnerable women which I think may feel uneasy about the idea. I run an all-women's organisation so I am very familiar with the women I come across."

"I fully understand, but I can assure you that I am very sensitive to their requirements and will try and make them feel as relaxed as possible."

"Okay. I guess I don't have any other option. I've brought this young lady Cynthia who would like a test done, as well as handing in these forms of women who will need referring."

"I'll get to working on them as soon as I have done Cynthia's examination."

"Thank you," Coleen said.

"Cynthia could you lie down on this bed please? Whilst I ask you a few questions," the male nurse said.

I lay myself on the bed, with my back upright, awaiting the questions.

"I want to firstly ask are you okay with... Sorry I didn't ask your name," turning to face Coleen.

"Coleen."

"Are you okay with Coleen being present while I conduct your tests?"

"Yes, that's fine with me," I said.

"Okay I will start. So today I'll be testing you in several ways for STI's this will be by urine, blood and swab samples. Are you happy for them to be done?"

"Yes."

"I'm now going to ask you a series of questions to know your history and be able to know if there are any further testing, or precautions that'll need to be done beforehand. Please be as honest as you can, my job is not to be judgemental, I do this all the time."

I say, "Okay," and smile.

"Have you had any symptoms prior to your visit today?"

"None."

"When was the last time you had any form of sexual activity?"

"A few days ago."

"What kind of sexual activity, oral, vaginal, anal?"

"Vaginal and oral."

"Was it protected?"

"No."

"Do you have one or more sexual partners?"

"I have one at the moment."
"How many have you had in the last six months?"

"About five."

"Were they of the opposite sex or different?"

"They were all of the opposite sex."

"Were they all protected?"

"They were, other than two which includes my most recent sexual partner."

"Did you have any testing done for STI's for the other partner you had in the past six months?"

"Yes, I did."

"As I've got all the answers I require, I will need you to unclothe your entire bottom half and cover yourself with the bed roll. Please lie back on the bed. We'll leave you to undress, let us know when you're ready."

He pulled the curtain around my bed as he and Coleen remained on the other side.

When I had done what he'd instructed, I said, "I'm ready."

The nurse pulled back the curtain and they both came around my bed.

"Okay, I'm going to put a speculum in your vaginal passage I want you to remain relaxed and take in a deep breath, it may feel uncomfortable but I'm going to do it as quickly but as gently as possible."

I lay there, feeling uncomfortable as he takes the swabs but loosen up as he gradually pulls it away.

"Okay I'm going to press here to see if your womb is okay."

Before he could lay his hand on me I said, "I don't have one."

"I see. Sorry to pry, have you had a hysterectomy then?"

"Yes."

"May I ask what happened?"

"I've lived without it for many years now, so I don't find it too hard to talk about now."

I did find it difficult to come to terms with it at the beginning as it all happened at once.

A girl called Linda and her friends beat me up and stabbed me when I was young, they ruptured my ovaries and caused internal bleeding whilst I was unconscious. The medical staff said that they had no other option but to give me a total hysterectomy.

As a teenager I didn't think, when I become an adult would I want kids the biological way, as at the time I knew it was never going to be an option for me in the future.

When I told snowflake in conversation, when we were talking about having a family, he said that that there were always other options like adoption which was a great alternative to bring up a child who needed us more and felt we had chosen them because they were special. It was good to know he accepted my situation and he was open to adoption. I'd not conjured up the courage to tell him I was adopted, as I thought there is only so much he'd accept of me, plus I didn't want to give him reason to give up on me like my parents.

"Here are some condoms for safe sex," said the nurse.

As the nurse and Coleen came out of my cubicle and pulled round the curtain, I heard the nurse to Coleen,

"Can I take you out some time for food?"

"Like a date?"

"If that's okay with you?"

"I'm not sure."

I interrupt shouting through the curtain, "What is there to think about? Girl got to eat, right?"

"Hmmm, I guess so," said Coleen.

"Don't feel like you're being pressured into something you don't want to, it's okay," said the nurse.

"Is it okay to take your number and I can think about it?" replied Coleen.

"Course, whatever you need," he says.

"Thanks," as she passes him her phone and he types his number in it.

"It's saved as, 'give me a chance',"

Coleen looks up to him and smiles, "Just maybe."

"Well it wasn't a no," the male nurse answered. "Means there's still hope."

As we finished off at the clinic, Coleen gives her pleasantries to the staff for all their help and then we leave.

When we were out the vicinity, I looked at Coleen waiting for her to realise I was watching her.

"What?" she said.

"What was all that about?" I said.

"Am I missing something?" Coleen asked.

"There was a premium guy ready to fine dine you, and you turned him down. What's wrong with you? Are you even going to even try and give him a chance? He probably already thinks you won't, bless him."

"I'm just not interested in seeing any one at the moment."

"Recent bad break up? Fill me in! I don't understand why not?"

"I just don't have a high regard in men. I don't believe I'm set up to find that guy who will have it all, the career mindset, charm and tender loving care for me."

"You say that, but the nurse to me had all the above, and he was so gentle and understanding with me. Come on now, you need to get in there before it's too late."

"I've heard this so many times at the Centre. How old are you? Are you single? Do you have kids? You're that old and you still haven't got kids. Tick, tock, times running out. Why does everyone think, you got to have kids by a certain age?"

"Okay calm down, I was just saying, not like I would understand."

"Sorry, sorry, that was totally insensitive of me. It just frustrates me, with the pressure you can be under like it's anyone else's business."

"Don't worry I was only pulling your leg."

"Okay, because of my insensitivity I won't agree to meet up with him as yet, but I'll text him, this is my number."

"You're so dry, like my ends right now," touching the ends of my hair.

"Here's me flaunting the goodies, there's you, keeping them dusty like artefacts. They're, there to be used."

"I'm not going to rush to have sex, until the time is right. My female gentalia is very precious and should be protected. When I find someone, and we both love each other, and decide as two consenting adults that this is what we want, then yes."

"Is that just a posh way of you saying, you're still a virgin Coleen?"

"Yes, but I still stand by what I say."

"Whhhat. No way, you're good. No wonder."

"I'm literally waiting for that one I'm certain is going to be the perfect one for me."

"I don't want to burst your bubble but Mr. Right for you, won't be perfect, but if you're able to work together and compromise with one another you could potentially make a good team. It's all about not putting too much expectations on each other and having common goals."

"I completely understand what you're getting at, now tell me why you're not settled down with your Mr. Right now?"

"Girl, I'm having way too much fun, for all of that. Let me work this pum pum until otherwise."

"You're way too much for me."

"You know you love the way I talk dirty," as I roll my tongue in her face. "Serious talk though Coleen, from my third eye, I could only feel warmth from the male nurse. There's definitely a magnetic force drawing, 'give me a chance' to you. Just tell him you'll accept a date."

"You've convinced me, I'll give him a chance."

"Thank God. That was hard work, but it worked."

"Okay so what you going to message him?"

"Hang on, I don't want to look desperate. Let me at least wait for a reply and have a bit of text chat."

"Well don't wait too long, man like night nurse, is on high demand Coleen."

"I can see I'm going to have great difficulty getting rid of you Cynthia."

"Of course, no escape now. I'll be like the herpes you've never had."

"Eurgh, gross Cynthia," said Coleen screwing her face up in disgust. "Well, just wanted to paint a realistic picture for you?" chuckled Cynthia.

THE BLOOD OBSESSION

"How has your week been?"

"Productive."

"Have you had any thoughts return from when we last spoke?"

"No."

"What do you believe you did differently why they haven't?"

"I'm not too sure. My routine practically is the same every day."

"Where do you see these sessions going, if you can't give me something to work with? It really makes my job very difficult Coleen."

"As long as I believe they're working, I will pay you for the service. I've been having these sessions long enough to know how it works."

"Okay, but if I think that we're not getting anywhere with them, I will need to be honest with you. It's not just about the money."

"I'll be honest. I go to the Centre where I'm helping women, and each time I listen to their stories, it all boils down to men. The treatment they've had to endure, their experiences it makes me sick. The thoughts then begin to creep in of wanting to self-harm, so I can feel what they're feeling and be part of their situation. I feel a hatred towards their perpetrators as how could you behave towards a woman in that manner. A woman needs care, love, warm attention but they don't seem to receive it."

"You need to understand that you can't control people's actions or what they've gone through. You need to be able to separate yourself from the equation, you are there to listen, just like I am to you. You are there to show them hope and how they can move forward to believe that they are free from their past. Their past is their past, and in the past and it cannot be changed, but the actions they take from that point on, they are in control of. They are in control of their destiny and what and who they bring into their life. They need to, including you, surround themselves with positive people, positive energy, let go of matters which are bringing negativity."

"I understand what you're saying to me, it's just very difficult. I get consumed by all that I hear, and I feel that I am the only one that can help, can understand and I want to be that person for them."

"Do you think that it would be a good idea, for you to come away from the Centre to focus on you?"

"No, definitely not. This is my calling, I just need to be able to, as you said, learn to separate my feelings from my work and not make it personal. I am helping these women and in turn it is helping me, understand myself and what I need to do, to work on myself."

"In your own time as homework then, write some tasks where you can work on you. It can be having a relaxing bath, meditation, walking in a park. At the end of the day, tell yourself what went well and what you're proud of yourself for achieving. You will slowly feel satisfied with small accomplishments."

"I will work on it and see how it goes."

"Same time next week? We've actually come to the end of your session."

"Yes, thank you. I'll put it in my diary."

"Take care of yourself Coleen, great session."

It's such a relief to come out of her office, it gets so tense when she starts trying to prod deeper and I don't feel I have the answers to her questions, they're just thoughts and feelings in my head. I know I got to let them out, but I still don't think I've got the grasp of it, when I'm so used to being on the other side, listening and taking in everyone else's thoughts and feelings.

I know everything I'm feeling is down to years of issues I've bottled up about my perceptions of men. I haven't had a male model around to teach me what the typical man should be like, only my opinions of what I've seen and heard from everyone else. I don't have any memories of my Father to know what we may have done together to know if he would have been a good father. My assumptions between him and my Mother's relationship was that he must have been very abusive and when his anger got the better of him, he lost control and killed her.

My Mother was gentle, kind, everything I remember a Mother should be. The way she used to comb and plait my hair ready for school on a Sunday night is etched on my memory. She would gently part my hair, oil my scalp, and then plait it to perfection. She also had the neatest dressing room table, all laid with various ceramic printed jewellery boxes, moisturisers and perfumes. I loved this one particular bottle, it had a pink tassel pump connected to it. When she'd emptied the contents, I'd spray it, so I could feel the air come from it with a slight aroma of what the scent was. She let me keep it as she knew how much I loved it; one of the few treasures I have to remember her by.

It's a constant pressure to keep these happy memories to the front of my mind, as they can get cloudy with the last images I saw of the blood dripping from her mouth as she lay motionless on the floor, her eyes focused, no blinks, just staring into a fixated angle with no hope of the wind to change them back. I didn't scream, I just stood there as her blood went drip drop just like a tap not tightened. The house was calm, not even my Father made a sound, as he walked straight past me still clutching the knife, without a glance back. It was like I was invisible, whilst he was in a trance. From the recollection of others, I've been told I was sitting in her blood until the medics and my Grandmother came and found me. I was clinging onto her body, pyjamas dyed in her fluid just silent.

I hate him. I lost the one that would teach me all she knew from cooking, sewing, giving me advice about boys, everything in the way she wanted to teach me, in her own special way. My Grandmother, my Mothers Mum whom I called Ma, did her best and I'm grateful for her taking on the responsibility of bringing me up; cooking some good soul food to make sure I had meat on my bones, making sure my clothes were clean and ironed so when I was old enough, I would be capable to do it myself, but it wasn't the same. I was unable to keep in touch with my Father's family after it happened and it was only Mother and Ma on our side as Mother was her only child and Pa had died before I was born from an aneurysm. I had a reasonable upbringing considering the circumstances, I got a career and began working. I just hadn't fulfilled the making a family part, which was not on the cards to have in the traditional way as I'd then have to have a man, so my choice would be adoption or IVF.

I lost both my parents that night, my Father went to prison but later died from an unexpected inmate incident. I didn't care for the details, it wouldn't be making a difference on how I was going to proceed for the future. Good ridents!

After what I'd witnessed I needed to have sessions with a psychiatrist regularly, to monitor my behaviour, show me how to express what I was feeling with imagery, as well as recording a diary about my daily activities.

I was told that I used to use my Mum as my imaginary companion. If I set the table I'd set the table with an extra place for her, if we were going anywhere I'd do the seatbelt in the car for her, all my actions involved her by my side. As I got older and started to realise that my mother had really gone, it became harder for me to cope with the fact that she wasn't ever coming back.

I'd rummaged in Ma's belongings one day when I was thirteen years old and found a box which included all the contents of what happened that dreadful night, the photos, post mortem, letters from my father in prison. It was the photos that stuck in my mind, I didn't get the chance to read the details of anything else as Ma interrupted me, snatching everything from me saying, they were not for my eyes and I had no right snooping in her possessions. I didn't see this box or the contents of it again, Ma made sure I wouldn't.

The psychiatrist and my Grandmother from then were very worried for my mental state as they believed it had conjured up past memories that had been hidden. I'd processed what I'd seen, and I would frequently self-harm when I had an opportunity, until I could see the blood appear from the incision. I was unable to be left alone in my room by myself for some time, as they worried for my safety and what I could get hold of to repeat the harming.

I was told that they were not surprised as when the traumatic event had happened I was five years old I would persistently bite myself or deliberately hurt myself, so I could shed blood and now that I was older it would be more fatal as I knew what I was doing. I can remember sitting at the bottom of the doctor's bed staring at the clock on the wall as the little hand went by, a second at a time, tick, tick, tick, whilst they changed my bandaged wrists nearly every week. It was a blessing there was never anything too serious like slitting a critical artery, or I wouldn't be here to tell the tale.

The feeling I had though was indescribable, I felt like I was back with my Mother at the time it happened. As I got a little hand-held blade and pierced it into my skin and saw the blood, I felt like I was transported back to the time it all happened. I could smell, picture even taste everything how it was. I had a hope that each time I could feel the scratch on my wrists I could feel what my Mother was feeling, the ability to see the droplets and reenact what I experienced that day and maybe with some bizarre trickle of hope, we were back in time like a renaissance and there was the ability to bring her back to life.

I continued to have therapy throughout my teenage years to adulthood to calm my nerves and maintain normality. When I was at primary school I was socially awkward and didn't have any friends. My Mother died as I was due to start primary school, so that's when my imaginary companion began to follow me, so it was difficult to connect with my classmates as my imaginary friend needed to accompany me. My classmates of course at that age thought it was weird and would laugh at me and say, 'You can't play with us,' so it was just my imaginary friend (Mother) and me in the playground, lunchtime to home time.

When it came to secondary school there was no improvement, my social skills were nil as I had not actively made any interactions with people in school, around my neighbourhood or the local church I attended with Ma. I didn't get involved in any activities as my peers would, I'd just kept company with myself. The other kids weren't exactly mean to me, they'd stare and whisper things about me amongst themselves and not include me in class discussions but that's as harmful as it got.

The transference or further rationalism to self-harming in my adolescence, was also a comfort mechanism, to allow myself to feel like I was still present in my body. As I did not participate in anything with my peers I sometimes felt like I was invisible, pupils would brush past me in the corridors or knock my bag off my shoulder without a murmur of sorry, so I needed confirmation from the self-harming that I was real. I was lonely, very lonely not being able to talk or relate to anyone my own age.

When the medical team found out my problem was psychological rather than medical, I changed to having a psychotherapist. My Ma and her would urge me to talk about what was going on inside my head but I didn't want to talk to them, I didn't have anything to say.

I of course wanted to have friends, be popular to some extent, go to school discos but I didn't have the confidence or the know-how. What past the time for me, was reading in my room, I could sink in to another reality with a good book. I enjoyed novels about romance, the fairytales of the one no one expected could get the Prince, did.

In addition to my lack of social status, my lack of attention to myself image was an issue that I didn't try to fix. I looked after myself hygienically, but in terms of ever plucking my eyebrows and putting the straighteners to my hair, was unimaginable. I had no sense of dress, I did live with my Ma, so she taught me how she would have behaved towards my Mother; to wear under skirts under my actual skirt, needing it to be past my knee, and my shoes, let's leave all that for your imagination.

The psychotherapist did help me to some extent, as she would give me tasks to look on at home by myself such as Maslow's hierarchy of needs, and glancing at how until different needs are met you will be unable to move onto the top level of self fulfilment. This is when I decided that when I'd leave school I'd study Psychology, as I would be able to learn in more depth about such a complex subject which seemed so bewildering. I admit, it was intense finding out so much about the mind and why people behaved the way they did. My therapy was much needed at this point, there was no way I'd have been able to cope with the complexity of the subject on a whole, solely, alone with my thoughts. It made me think how I was as a person, how I felt neglected, which brought on the suicidal thoughts as I didn't have answers to my why questions along with, I may be alone for the rest of my life.

It was hard to explain how I felt at times. It was like, there was no feelings, but the tears continued to fall from my eyes and I didn't know why. I used to sit on the couch and sit there just staring into space, wondering were things ever going to change and answering the question in my head, that it wouldn't. I'd been on this earth for so long already and what did I have to show; a few certificates to show I was qualified in a particular subject. I'd walk to the kitchen and it remained the same... Emptiness. I would be missed if I was gone, but not for long.

I had to pretend that I was not in my actual reality, close my eyes and think what my dream reality would be, feel like, just like the stories I'd read, so I could try be rid of some of the pain of not wanting to be alive.

It felt calming knowing that the dream reality felt genuine at that time, disappearing with no problems, no fears, no nothing. It may sound bizarre to you, but it made sense to me.

When I finished my degree I was so happy, I had a feeling of accomplishment. Though my Mother wasn't there to see, I still wanted to make her proud, I didn't want her to look down on me and see me as a disappointment.

I then had to think, well what would I do with my new achievement. I knew that for the long term being in a workplace setting, I wouldn't necessarily build on my psychological needs of finding new friends as they were usually set up of cliques and that was not what I was accustomed to.

There was a building in my neighbourhood that I grew up in, which had become derelict. It was of a sufficient size, not too big or small, and was used for a community Centre at a time. When I got home one evening, (I still lived with Ma), I spoke to her and told her I had an idea about establishing a Centre for women which I'd dedicate in the memory of my Mother, so anyone who felt alone could come and feel safe. She thought it was a good idea and said to make sure I knew how to sustain the running costs, as buying the property, (once knew who it'd belonged to), wouldn't be a problem, as I had been left money from my Mother's will when she died.

It was an easier task than I expected, finding out who owned the property and purchasing it. The difficult tasks were in the complete renovation, in making it health and safety proof and ensuring I had the right policies in place once it was open. I really had to step out of my comfort zone to get the Centre up and running, I firstly got an article in the newspaper to announce the opening and all was welcome but at the opening there would be strict security guidelines in terms of men accessing the building, as the women attended needed to feel safe.

The open day went well, I actually accumulated various numbers for volunteers, women who wanted to put on classes for fitness and crafts and who wanted to give funding for external referrals for me to take on clients for therapy. This move felt surreal, I was going to be able to have a career but also potentially have clients and friends. The complimentary service I started called 'Freedom to Speak' which I ran daily, was a big hit and users felt a sense of relief off-loading their problems as well as hearing what others had experienced which was often similar.

When I had set up a pop-up service area which I had jointly done with a local sexual health clinic to help raise awareness, I met Cynthia as you already know. What is unknown is that she was the first person I can say was someone I felt I could trust and believe was my friend who was not directly connected to work, as we started to get to know each other outside of YANA. She wanted to know me for me and we had more in common than we realised, not knowing our parents, the difficulty of not knowing who we were, being bullied to name a few. She gave me comfort which I had never felt before, that feeling of someone who genuinely cared for your wellbeing and what you're up to.

As Cynthia was there when I initially met Idris (night nurse), she made sure I was ready for my first ever date, and what an exciting time I had in getting ready for it.

"Okay so have you got any idea what you want to wear to your first date with night nurse?" says Cynthia.

"Well I was thinking..." As I pull something from my wardrobe very slowly and embarrassingly.

"Wow, omg, no Coleen no. I'm sorry but that looks like your Ma's curtains. How? What? Why? When? It doesn't actually matter, you're not wearing it, and if that was the best outfit you had in your closet, all of it has gotta go," Cynthia acting frantic by the shock.

"I have you now, so you can help me, rather than criticising my vintage pieces. Yes?"

"I guess so, if I knew they'd be so much work to do I'd have come around earlier, good job I brought an emergency kit just in case."

"An emergency kit?"

"Yup, a hot comb to tame the fro, pair of tweezers, shavers, nail file, nude nail polish, head scarf, dresses, wedges, you get my drift?"

"You came prepared."

"Damn right, your coochie got bats flying from it, time for butterflies."

"You're something else," as I put my hand on my head and shake my head in shame.

"Yes. I'm going to transform you from an ugly duckling to a swan, no offence," as Cynthia holds up one particular dress.

"None taken, I understand what you're getting at."

"Okay let's begin."

She begins to do my hair, parting it in sections. We did it in the kitchen, so we could put the comb on the hob fire. I'd never used one of these before, they were made of brass with a wooden handle and heated on the hob fire to get hot. Cynthia said it would be better than straighteners as I'd never had heat on my hair like that before and she wanted to tame it not make it look dead straight. I had to keep still whilst she did my hair, so the hot comb wouldn't touch my scalp or ears. To cool it down she'd press it on a damp towel from side to side. When she finished she did two plaits around the crown of my head, it looked really nice and tidy.

"I think we need to get some music up in here, get you in the mood, what you got?"

She looks over to where I point, to see my vinyl record player.

"You must be kidding me. You're definately vintage I'll give you that, but a few upgrades babe won't hurt. What artists you got for me?"

"Minnie Riperton, The Isley Brothers, Etta James, James Brown."

"Okay just stop! Let's settle for YouTube on the phone."

"These used to be my Mothers, so I got used to listening to them for an understanding of what she was like."

"No need to explain, I can see where you're coming from. If I had an inch of what my birth parents could have left behind for me, I'd be the same. They're some classics don't get me wrong, but not the kind of classics I'd like to get you in the right mood for tonight.

I finish getting ready, with an application of mascara and natural lipstick to complete. I looked amazing and didn't feel like I had changed who I was, Cynthia had spruced me up in a way that I was contemporary. The dress I wore was just above the knee, forest green, flower printed with a side tie wrap and some wedged tan shoes to compliment.

"Yes girl, you are killing it. He is not going to be able to take his eyes off you."

"Thank you, I really appreciate you taking out the time to be here for me."

"That's what friends are for. Come on bring it in," as she gives me a hug.

"Now you enjoy yourself and relax and be sure to tell me all the details when you're finished."

"Okay I will," escorting her to the door to leave my house.

It wasn't too long after that my taxi ended up coming to pick me up to take me to the restaurant. I was so nervous, but I continued to breathe in and out and reassure myself that I was going to have a good night.

When I got to the restaurant which was very classy, the waiter escorted me to the table Idris was sitting at, waiting for me.

He stands up to pull out my seat for me to sit on. As I sit, and he helps me bring my chair in, to then work his way around the table to seat himself in his chair.

"So, you made it then?"

"I did, indeed."

"You look absolutely beautiful. I'm happy you changed your mind to consider my proposal of meeting."

"I can't say it was easy, but I am too, glad to be here."

"Don't you do this often?"

"This, like dinner date? No no no."

"I decline most men, if they're even able to even get that far in the conversation with me."

"What caused you to be this way towards men?"

"I've not come across many decent men, and with the work I do, I see and hear far few."

"What about your Father?"

"He's dead."

"Okay, sorry to hear."

"Don't be, he murdered my Mother and later died in prison."

"I see, it's all starting to make more sense now."

"How old were you, when this happened?"

"About five years old. There were extracts of it all that stayed with me of the night my Mother died, but I've had to have therapy to help me through this."

"Sorry to hear."

"Could we come off this subject, it's starting to get a little morbid. We're starting to get to know each other and this is supposed to be a nice meal for two in a fancy restaurant, let's enjoy."

"Deal."

"Tell me about your parents?"

"My mum lives in Nigeria, I will visit her when I can and... My Father's dead."

"Sorry to hear... Okay let's not talk about family and stick to where we've possibly travelled and where we'd want to go, is that okay with you?"

"Good idea," he says and the both of us start to laugh.
I enjoyed my first official date ever. He was unlike the perceptions I had of him, he was calm, a good listener, very open unlike myself in general. We even closed the evening with him kissing me on the cheek and him asking if we could do it again. I told him, I'd very much like that. It was time for me to bring down the barriers of stopping anyone in and allow the happiness that I could potentially have in store, come forth.

ALL LIES IN A BOX

The day had started with Cynthia accompanying me to Celine's court case. It was a very sad verdict in which I knew Caroline would later need our support for. I departed ways with Cynthia at the court and said I'd meet her at 'Freedom to Speak' later on this afternoon as I wanted to go visit Ma and go home and change.

When I got back, Ma was home. I was unable to touch base with her in the morning as the case was put on early, so I was glad we would be able to catch up before I headed back out.

"How's your day been sweetheart?" Ma said.

"It didn't start too great for one of the women who attend my sessions Ma. She found out that her friend who tried to defend her from the man who raped her, was found guilty and sentenced to imprisonment for accidentally killing him."

"Oh, dear child, that's very sad to hear."

"I know, I feel very saddened as her friend had also attended my sessions at the Centre with her previously and was hoping to change her life after an abusive relationship resulted in her children being taken from her."

"This world we're living in can be such a bad place, but we have to keep believing it can only get better Leeney."

"Yes Ma."

"What was the name of that dreadful man? I don't recall reading it in the newspaper."

"There was an article produced in the newspaper, his name was Campbell Jackson."

"Come again, Campbell Jackson?"

"Ma. Do you know who he is?"

Ma didn't reply but got up and left the room and returned with a box and said I think it's time child."

I looked at the box she presented on the breakfast table and it looked familiar for some reason.

"I feel like I recognise this box Ma, what is it?"

"You stumbled on it when you were thirteen years old it contained confidential information I didn't want you to know at the time."

"Okay I'm intrigued, continue."

"It's for you to inspect. Be cautious."

I opened the box and started to take out its contents one at a time. I took out the brown file which had confidential printed in red on the outside, it had photos inside of a bloody body, in what I assumed was my Mother's. There were different viewpoints, closeups of her injuries which included foot prints of where I walked away from her blood. as well as where I sat as she lay there. There was a post mortem analysis report which detailed how many times she was stabbed and where. As I dug deeper I saw letters unopened from my Father in prison, and then another set of letters that had been opened but different handwriting. As I began to read each one at a time, puzzled, put it back it in its original envelope and reached for another, I became nervier. This didn't make any sense to me.

I couldn't speak, I was speechless. I couldn't fathom anything. The truth lay in this box the whole time and only now I was finding out. I had to go. The women were expecting me, and I couldn't let them down, I needed to be there.

When I got to the Centre, Cynthia was there to greet me. She asked, "Are you okay?"

"Yes yes, I'll talk to you after," I said.

"Sounds ominous, you definately don't sound yourself."

"I don't feel like it either, but I need to conduct this session and then relieve my suppression."

"Okay, I'm here for you."

We take our seats and wait as each of our ladies came in and took a seat also. We start as a woman begins to speak, I don't even know what she was saying, but I was alert enough to see when Caroline walked in the room looking distraught.

When the lady had finished, Cynthia speaks, "I'm not ready to talk about my life as yet, but I'd like to share a few words from a poem I wrote. Don't look at me with that disapproving look, were you there? Did you see? Or was it just hear say? Don't look at me with those judgie eyes, did you go through it? What would you have done? Don't look at me, without staring me straight beneath my eyes, the pain I try to hide to conquer each day. Thank you."

I speak and say, "Have we got anyone else who wants to share?"

Caroline to my surprise, puts her hand up and begins to speak. I again zone out, running events in my head of what I'd read, seen, then my ears perk up when Caroline gets to the point in which she says, "The revelation is, is that not only do I know who my Father is, he is the supposed victim of the murder plus attempted rape on myself. To top it off, my friend who is in trouble and charged with the offence, is my half-sister. Tell me what do I do with news like that? As I sure don't know."

When I hear this, there was silence, no one in the room knew what to say. I then spoke to break the stillness, "What you need to do is embrace your sister with open arms. The situation has brought pain upon you both, but it has also brought upon your happiness which you didn't expect. In our lives we are confronted with truths we can't understand why, but there is a reason, so we can learn, grow and share to support others as well as ourselves. Thank you for sharing Caroline, if you could stay behind after the session I'd like you to speak with me."

As we end the session, the ladies as the usual routine, help themselves to refreshments. When the room became empty I ask Caroline and Cynthia to come with me.

"You okay Caroline?" I asked.

"I'm not, I'm in shock. I don't know what my next plan of action is," Caroline replies.

"I can understand where you're coming from," I say.

"How? What do you know about betrayal and your whole life being a lie? It's easy for you to say, you come here every day and listen to everyone's problems with an answer to everything to solve our problems, meanwhile you go back to your happy little life."

"What do you know Caroline? Really, about my life? You've come here seeing a half-finished product of what I began from the loneliness, depression amongst everything else I've endured not having anyone to support me. I started this without even knowing this would even work, I just knew I had to, as I was sick of being alone. Cynthia here is the first person I can call a friend my entire life, after meeting her in town and starting this Centre a year ago. So, what do you know about my happy little life? I lived with my Grandmother until recently at the age of twenty-six and have no Mother or Father, so when I say I understand, I understand. I did want to talk to you on a level but I'm unsure if you are able to handle it."

"I'm sorry Coleen, I'm angry and I feel alone, you've been a support to me just like Celine has, which I didn't imagine receiving and I just assumed that everything was perfect for you."

"Well I'm here to tell you, it far from is. As I said to you Cynthia I would talk to you after about what was bothering me, but you need to be here also Caroline as it involves you too."

"Okay," Caroline looking confused.

"After the court case I went home and saw my Ma and we talked, and she revealed a box to me. The box had various items in it about my Mother and her life before I was born. It showed me a few revelations too... My Father killed my Mother as he had found out that my Mother had lied to him that I wasn't his daughter his brother was, and my Mother wasn't as nice as I thought she was, she was a conniving, manipulative woman who was out for what she could get."

"So how does this involve me then Coleen?" Caroline asks.

"Well my real Father as well as yours is Campbell."

"What the @%!? Are you serious? This shit is not making no sense? So now I have three sisters I was unaware of," Caroline says.

"What do you mean three?" I said.

"My Mother when wanting to relay her wrongs like she was on her death bed, slipped in I had a twin who was darker than me and had to be adopted as my racist grandparents wouldn't have condoned it."

Cynthia remaining quiet throughout all this, absorbing our mix up conversation, she intervenes, "It might seem weird me asking but being the outsider throughout this, I'm feeling the universe has brought us all together for a reason. What is your birth date Caroline?"

"18th July 1993," Caroline and Cynthia both say together.

"Oh my gosh," Cynthia cries.

"If you only knew how I'd been struggling with who I am, my whole identity and you're standing here with the key to unlock what's been missing."

Caroline moves towards Cynthia and comforts her, "I've felt like I've been missing something my whole entire life too."

"Not anymore... Coleen, come on bring it in, you're our Sister too," Cynthia holds out her arm to me, so we can all feel united together.

Caroline breaks up the hug and says, "This changes everything. There must be some way in which the case can be dropped for Celine, due to the circumstances. We have to tell her the good news, she'll be shocked but so happy. Let me call her solicitor."

Caroline calls her solicitor. She isn't on the phone for too long, as she comes off, she looks at us and says, "She's dead."

"What?" I said.

"He told me, that the prison had called to say that she'd hung herself in her cell," Caroline weeps.

"Caroline, I'm so sorry," I said.

"So am I," said Cynthia.
"All I know is that her death can't be in vain," ends Caroline.

WE ALL ARE OUR SISTERS KEEPER

So you've heard our stories our journeys, but that's not the end as you can see for us. I Cynthia, adopted Kayla and her brother Paul Jnr. and we all collectively bring them up together as a family. We came together to produce, A Womans Worth Convention so that we could share with you, that you're not alone and that whatever you're going through, to remind yourself what is your worth? How much do you value yourself? Do not compromise who you are for no one, if in doubt re read your twenty-five commandments. We helped each other initially as we had something in common with our circumstances when in actual fact we were connected by blood. The thing is we would always be sisters even if we didn't know, as we all are, our sister's keeper with the common denominator being a woman. As you evaluate each of our stories, take from them individually what it meant. Celine may have committed suicide, but it didn't mean the end for Kayla's life. I hope you take from today, as a revelation, for reflection with resolutions.

I take back the power that was stolen from me, by the empowerment of my strength I gain from shared experiences of mine and others. The old me is gone I cut all ties of the old me. That is not me. I want to bring forth the me, that wants to represent who I am as a woman, that though I may have had traumas in my life, I won't let that define who I am. I am going to arise and inspire to be myself, live my dreams and grow through struggles, truly inspired to wear the invisible badges of strength, confidence, courage, compassion, and fearlessness.

A.W.W CONVENTION WORSHEETS

RESOLUTION

Create a positive mantra you can tell yourself each day like the YANA pledge

…..

…..

....

…..

....

....

Name three things you want for yourself in life?

1…..

2..

3..

Do you want them now or need them now? If it is a want, why do believe you want them now? What could you do whilst you wait for what you want?

…………………………………………………………………………………

…………………………………………………………………………………

…………………………………………………………………………………

…………………………………………………………………………………

…………………………………………………………………………………

…………………………………………………………………………………

…………………………………………………………………………………

What goals will need to be in place to achieve them?

What is the goal?	Time for completion	How will you achieve goal?

Produce a chart of tasks what you need to do each day that will help improve your lifestyle?

LAST THOUGHTS FROM AUTHOR

I came up with three words beginning with 'E' delievered as acrostic poems to close. These three words are educate, enrichment, and entertainment.

Elevate like a soaring plane and fly

Distinguishing the fact from fiction with knowledge

Undertake testing to access what your mind has absorbed

Captivating your audiences' minds with mastery

Absorb their constructive criticism to accentuate

Thought provoking questions which will further

Educate, unlocking the power to lead and empower

Enhance the mind and body with,

Neuro linguistic programming

Reflexology and reiki to name a few methods that will

Improve your life and,

Challenge your weaknesses, so

Habits become routine like hypnosis

Mentally, physically and emotionally

Enriching a lifestyle that once was hidden, but

Now discovered through

Therapy techniques, rhetorically practiced sharing and pass on

Enjoyment comes in many forms to excite the spirit

Negativity extracted from the equation and put aside, as only

Tolerance of good vibes, banter and laughter are allowed

Excessive drinking, if can act responsibly. As

Repercussions for certain actions cannot be reversed

Tailored suits and couture dresses to empress the eye at prestigious events

Amusement encouraged at the circus, fairs and theme parks

Inventions of all kinds for games at home or special occasions

Non-conventional activities are thriving in an industry some would not condone

Music playing creating a party atmosphere

Energising the body as you show off your best dance moves

Nights of relaxation and letting your hair down

Thankful for the distractions from everyday life trials

I NEED HELP

The topics mentioned in this book can have long term damage, and the healing progress can be very hard to deal with, if the victim does not have the support network or unaware of where they can get the support from.

The companies who have kindly allowed us to print their contact details, have neither endorsed or had a role in any production of this book, and the sole purpose is to signpost readers to get help or more information for some of the issues raised in this book.

FPA CHARITY

We're a sexual health charity. We give straightforward information and support on sexual health, sex and relationships to everyone in the UK.

FPA sexual health enquiry service

Helpline Northern Ireland– 0345 122 8687 9am to 5pm Monday to Friday (except bank holidays).

Helpline England
We regret that our helpline closed due to lack of funding. You can call the National Sexual Health Helpline provided by Public Health England on 0300 123 7123 (Monday–Friday, 9am to 8pm)

TIME TO CHANGE

Time to Change is a growing social movement working to change the way we all think and act about mental health problems. We've already reached millions of people and begun to improve attitudes and behaviour.

Despite the progress we've made, we know that many people still don't consider mental health relevant to them. They don't believe mental health problems are likely to affect them or people they know.

But the reality is that mental health can affect anyone. Statistically, 1 in 4 of us will fight a mental health problem in any given year. That's why our work is so important. No one should have to fear being treated differently because of a mental health problem.

Email: info@time-to-change.org.uk
Tel: 020 8215 2356

MIND

Mind is a leading national mental health charity working for better mental health. You can find a range of information resources at mind.org.uk and contact the Mind info-line on 0300 1233393 (open 9am to 6pm, Monday to Friday)

YOUNG MINDS

We're the UK's leading charity fighting for children and young people's mental health. We're here to make sure they get the best possible mental health support and have the resilience to overcome life's difficulties.

Parents worried about a child

Speak to our experts at the Parents Helpline – call 0808 802 5544.

WOMENS AID

Women's Aid is a federation of over 220 organisations, that provide more than 300 local lifesaving services to women and children across the country. The 24hr freephone National Domestic Violence Helpline (run in partnership between Women's Aid and Refuge) is available on 0808 2000 247 24 hours a day, 7 days a week.'

If you want more information please see our website here: https://www.womensaid.org.uk/what-we-do/

RAPE CRISIS

Rape Crisis England & Wales is a feminist organisation that exists to promote the needs and rights of women and girls who have experienced sexual violence, to improve services to them and to work towards the elimination of sexual violence.

rapecrisis.org.uk

ADDACTION

We help people change their behaviour to become the very best that they can be. It could be their drug or alcohol use or worries about their mental health – we support people to make lasting change in their lives.

We deliver 81 services across England and Scotland. In 2017 we supported 140,000 people.

We work with adults and young people, in community settings, in prisons, in residential rehab and through outreach.

http://www.addaction.org.uk/

PAPYRUS

Hopeline UK

We provide confidential support and advice to young people and anyone worried about a young person

We run a national helpline, HOPELineUK, including text and email services, staffed by a team of mental health professionals who provide practical help and advice to vulnerable young people and to those concerned about any young person who may be at risk of suicide.

National Confidential Helpline – HOPELineUK

If you are a young person at risk of suicide or are worried about a young person at risk of suicide:

0800 068 41 41

Mon-Fri 10:00 am to 10:00 pm

Weekends 2:00 pm to 10:00 pm

Bank Holidays 2:00 pm to 10:00 pm

BROOK

Brook has been at the forefront of providing wellbeing and sexual health support for young people for over 50 years.
Brook has services across the UK providing free and confidential sexual health services to young people under 25.

https://www.brook.org.uk/

STATISTICS

The topics mentioned in this book are increasing problems which are impacting society in a big way especially the victims. This book I hope can make more people aware of the issues by the statistics stated below and prevent more women predominantly young women becoming statistics in these problem areas. There are around two million single parents – they make up nearly a quarter of families with dependent children.

- Less than two per cent of single parents are teenagers
- 67.1 per cent of single parents are in work
- The majority of single parents don't receive child maintenance payments
- 47 per cent of children in single parent families live in relative poverty, around twice the risk of relative poverty faced by children in couple families (24 per cent).
- The proportion of families with children headed by single parents has remained at around 25 per cent for over decade
- The proportion of single parents who are fathers has stayed at around 10 per cent for over ten years

- The proportion of single parents in work increased from 55.8 per cent to 64.4 per cent over the past decade

- Single parents' risk of poverty has fallen over the past decade, yet those in single parent families are still nearly twice as likely to be in poverty as those in couple parent families.

Source: Gingerbread Single parents, equal families published on 29 August 2018

SELF HARM

- More than a fifth of 14-year-old girls in the UK said they had self-harmed, a report suggests.

- A survey of 11,000 children found 22% of the girls and 9% of the boys said they had hurt themselves on purpose in the year prior to the questionnaire.

- Rates of self-harm were worst (46%) among those who were attracted to people of the same or both genders.

The data on self-harm was analysed by The Children's Society after being collected in 2015 in the Millennium Cohort Study, a continuing research project following the lives of 19,000 children born in the UK between 2000 and 2001.

More than 11,000 of these children answered a questionnaire about whether they had hurt themselves on purpose in any way in the past year. Out of the 5,624 girls who responded, 1,237 said they had self-harmed.

Based on the figures, The Children's Society estimates that 109,000 children aged 14 may have self-harmed across the UK during the 12-month period in 2015 - 76,000 girls and 33,000 boys.

It follows NHS data released this month that showed the number of admissions to hospital of girls aged 18 and under for self-harm had almost doubled in two decades, from 7,327 in 1997 to 13,463 in 2017.

Source: BBC NEWS 29 August 2018

DOMESTIC ABUSE

Domestic abuse in England and Wales: year ending March 2017

- An estimated 1.9 million adults aged 16 to 59 years experienced domestic abuse in the last year, according to the year ending March 2017 Crime Survey for England and Wales (1.2 million women, 713,000 men).

- The police recorded 1.1 million domestic abuse-related incidents and crimes in the year ending March 2017 and of these, 46% were recorded as domestic abuse-related crimes; domestic abuse-related crimes recorded by the police accounted for 32% of violent crimes.

- There were 46 arrests per 100 domestic abuse-related crimes recorded by 39 police forces in the year ending June 2017.

- The majority of victims of domestic homicides recorded between April 2013 and March 2016 were females (70%).

- A decision to charge was made for 72% of domestic abuse-related cases referred to the Crown Prosecution Service (CPS) by the police, and of those that proceeded to court, convictions were secured for 76% of domestic abuse-related prosecutions.

There were 305 refuge services operating in England and Wales in 2017.A total of 83,136 high-risk cases were discussed at multi-agency risk assessment conferences in the year ending March 2017, equating to 36 cases per 10,000 adult females.

https://www.ons.gov.uk/peoplepopulationandcommunity/crim
eandjustice/bulletins/domesticabuseinenglandandwales/yearen
dingmarch2017

RAPE

Rape Crisis England & Wales headline statistics 2017-18:

- Rape Crisis Centres across our network responded to over 179,000 helpline calls during the year.

- Rape Crisis specialist services were accessed by 78,461 individuals an increase of 17% from 2016-17.

- Rape Crisis Centres provided in excess of 650,000 sessions of specialist support, including advocacy, emotional support and counselling, an increase of 44% since 2016-17.

- Three-quarters of all adult service users contacted Rape Crisis Centres about sexual violence that took place at least 12 months earlier; 42% were adult survivors of child sexual abuse

The largest group that contact Rape Crisis Centres, over half of service users are those who prefer to self-refer. This pattern has remained consistent over the past seven years and continues to demonstrate the necessity for funded independent services.

- 93 per cent of service users were female.

- Where age is known, 3,236 were aged 15 or under, an increase of 22% on last year; those aged under 25 represented 27% of service users.

- Where ethnicity is known, 23% of service users identified as Black or Minority Ethnic.

- 29% of all service users identified as Disabled.

- The Rape Crisis England & Wales website received over 12 million hits during the year - an increase of a third on 2016-17 - and an average of 46,850 unique visitors per month, a 43% rise from the previous year

Here are some other key statistics about sexual violence:

- Approximately 85,000 women and 12,000 men are raped in England and Wales alone every year; that's roughly 11 rapes (of adults alone) every hour. These figures include assaults by penetration and attempts.

- Nearly half a million adults are sexually assaulted in England and Wales each year

- 1 in 5 women aged 16 - 59 has experienced some form of sexual violence since the age of 16

- Only around 15% of those who experience sexual violence choose to report to the police

- Approximately 90% of those who are raped know the perpetrator prior to the offence

- 31% of young women aged 18-24 report having experienced

Sexual abuse in childhood (NSPCC, 2011)

In 2012-13, 22,654 sexual offences against under-18s were reported to police in England and Wales with four out of five cases involving girls (NSPCC, 2014)

- Most women in the UK do not have access to a Rape Crisis Centre (Map of Gaps, 2007)
- A third of people believe women who flirt are partially responsible for being raped (Amnesty, 2005)

Conviction rates for rape are far lower than other crimes, with only 5.7% of reported rape cases ending in a conviction for the perpetrator. (Kelly, Lovett and Regan, A gap or a chasm? Attrition in reported rape cases, 2005)

Source: https://rapecrisis.org.uk/statistics.php

CHILD ABUSE

- 1 in 20 children in the UK have been sexually abused
- Over 2,900 children were identified as needing protection from sexual abuse in 2015/16
- 1 in 3 children sexually abused by an adult did not tell anyone
- Over 90%of sexually abused children were abused by someone they knew

- Around a third of sexual abuse is committed by other children and young people
- 14% of contacts to the NSPCC's helpline last year were concerns about sexual abuse 2017
- Over 8,000 contacts to the NSPCC's helpline last year were concerns about sexual abuse 2017
- There were over 9000 counselling sessions with children and young people who talked to Childline in 2016/17 about sexual abuse

There were over 2,100 counselling sessions with young people who talked in Childline about online child sexual exploitation (CSE) in 2016/17

- Disabled children are more likely to be abused than non-disabled children
- Over 63,000 sexual offences against children were recorded by the police in the UK in 2016/17
- Nearly 30,000 registered offenders have been convicted of offences against children
- There were over 24,000 Childline counselling sessions with children about bullying in 2016/17
- More than 16,000 young people are absent from school due to bullying

Source: NSPCC

Drug misuse related hospital admissions (England)

- There were 7,545 hospital admissions with a primary diagnosis of drug-related mental health and behavioural disorders. This is 12 per cent lower than 2015/16 but 12 per cent higher than 2006/07

- There were 14,053 hospital admissions with a primary diagnosis of poisoning by illicit drugs. This is 7 per cent lower than 2015/16 but 40 per cent more than 2006/07.

- Deaths related to drug misuse (England and Wales)

- In 2016 there were 2,593 registered deaths in England and Wales related to drug misuse. This is an increase of 5 per cent on 2015 and 58 per cent higher than 2006

- Deaths related to drug misuse are at their highest level since comparable records began in 1993

Drug use among adults (England and Wales)

In 2016/17, around 1 in 12 (8.5 per cent) adults aged 16 to 59 in England and Wales had taken an illicit drug in the last year.

This level of drug use was similar to the 2015/16 survey (8.4 per cent), but is significantly lower than a decade ago (10.1 per cent in the 2006/07 survey).

Drug use among children (England)

In 2016, 24 per cent of pupils reported they had ever taken drugs. This compares to 15 per cent in 2014.

The likelihood of having ever taken drugs increased with age, from 11 per cent of 11-year old's to 37 per cent of 15-year old's.

https://digital.nhs.uk/dataandinformation/publications/statistical/statistics-on-drugmisuse/2018

LOOKED AFTER CHILDREN

On 31stMarch 2017:

- 72,670 children were in the care of local authorities
- The rate of looked after children per 10,000 children under 18 years was 62 Placements

On 31st March 2017:

- 74% (53,420) of children looked after were living with foster carer's
- 11% (7,890) were living in secure units, children's homes or hostels
- 6% (4,370) were placed with their parents
- 3% (2,520) were placed for adoption
- 4% (3,090) were with another placement in the community
- 2% (1,210) were placed in residential schools or other residential settings

Foster Placements

On 31stMarch 2017, of the 53,420 children in foster placements:

- 32,270 (62%) were placed inside the council boundary
- 8,830 (17%) were being fostered by a relative or friend
- 380 (1%) were in placements where the carer is also an approved adopter (fostering for adoption) or where they were subject to concurrent planning

Legal Status

On 31st March 2017:

- 50,470 children looked after under care orders
- 16,470 children looked after under voluntary agreements under Section 20 of Children's Act 1989
- 5,440 children looked after under placement orders

ADOPTION

Adoptions from Care

- 4,350 looked after children were adopted during the year ending 31 March 2017

Awaiting Adoption

- 3,720 children had an adoption decision but were not yet placed at 31 March 2017
- 2,470 children had a placement order for adoption but were not yet placed at 31 March 2017

Waiting Times

457 - the average number of days between a child entering care

and moving in with its adoptive family during the year 2016-2017

(Adoption scorecard indicator A1)

190 - the average number of days between an LA receiving court authority to place a child and the LA deciding on a match to an adoptive family during the year 2016-2017 (Adoption scorecard indicator A2)

Foster Carer Adoptions

Of the 2,520 looked after children who were placed for adoption at 31 March 2017, 260 were placed with their current foster carer

Adopter Characteristics

During year ending 31 March 2017:

- 90% (3,920) of children were adopted by couples and

- 10% (420) by single adopters.

- 9.7% (420) of children were adopted by same sex couples (either in a civil partnership, married or neither).

https://corambaaf.org.uk/fostering-adoption/lookedafter-

children-adoption-fostering-statistics/statistics-england

Adoption Match currently has 1106 children awaiting adoption, and 414 families waiting to adopt April 2016-March 2017

On the Adoption Register for England in the year April 2016 to

March 2017:

- 72% of children waiting to be adopted were 2 years and older

- 64% of children waiting to be matched were in sibling groups of two or more

- 56% of children waiting to be matched were boys and 44% of children waiting were girls

- 72% of children referred to the Adoption Register for England were white children and 28% were black minority ethnic children.

The Adoption Register for England hold 6 National Adoption

Exchange Days over 12 months on behalf of the Department for

Education. In the year April 2016 – March 2017:

- 126 children found permanent families through these events
- Nearly 1000 families have benefitted from these events and over 200 agencies

Children featured at these events are harder to place; children over 3 years old, of a BME ethnicity, part of a sibling group or with additional needs.

SUICIDE IN PRISON

There were 295 deaths in prison custody in the 12 months to

December 2017, down 17% from 354 in the previous year. Three of these were homicides, the same as the previous year. There were 70 self-inflicted deaths, down from 122 in the previous year, 2 of which were in the female estate, compared to 12 in the previous 12 months.

Self-harm reached a record high of 42,837 incidents in the 12

months to September 2017, up 12% from the previous year. The number of incidents requiring hospital attendance rose by 15% to 3,007. Quarterly self-harm incidents rose by 10% to a record high of 11,904 incidents.

Source: https://www.gov.uk/government/collections/safetyin-

custody-statistics

MENTAL HEALTH

Statistics for England

- An estimated 1 in 6 people experienced a 'common mental disorder' like depression or anxiety in the past week.

- Around 1 million people received psychological therapy for a common mental disorder through the IAPT programme in 2016/17

- Younger people, people living in deprived areas, and people with disabilities are all less likely than average to recover from their condition after psychological therapy.

- Waiting times for psychological therapy vary from 16 days in

- Waltham Forest to 167 days in Leicester (counting waits for both first and second treatment)

- 1 million people were in contact with adult mental health services as of December 2017

- Total spending on mental health was planned to be 11.9 billion in 2017/18- a 0.4% real terms increase on the previous year

Source: House of Commons Library Briefing Paper Number 6988, 25 April 2018

Mental health, learning disabilities and autism services

- At the end of March, there were 1,254,365 people in contact with services; the majority of these 1,012,781 were in adult mental health services.

- There were 195,271 people in contact with children and young people's mental health services and 85,395 in learning disabilities and autism services.

- 280,613 new referrals were received into services during March and 1,705,404 care contacts were attended.

- 20,961 people were subject to the Mental Health Act at the end of March, including 15,440 people detained in hospital.

- In the year between 1 April 2017 and 31 March 2018 there were 2,510,745 people in contact with services.

Of these; 573,270 were aged 18 years or less, 1,319,514 were aged between 19 and 64, and 616,796 were aged 65 years or more.

Of the people in contact with services between 1 April 2017 and 31 March 2018 103,952 had an inpatient spell.

Of these; 4,714 were aged 18 years or less, 78,883 were aged between 19 and 64, and 20,284 were aged 65 years or more.

Adult mental health services

- Between 1 January and 31 March 3,484 referrals with suspected first episode psychosis started treatment, of which 2,148 (61.7 per cent) waited two weeks or less.

- 77.8 per cent of people in contact with adult mental health services at the end of March who had been treated under the Care

Programme Approach for twelve months received a review during that time. There were 8,343 open ward stays at the end of March in adult acute mental health inpatient care, and 5,722 open ward stays in specialised adult mental health services.

Children and young people in contact with mental health services

- Between 1 January and 31 March 2,721 new referrals for people aged under 19 with eating disorder issues were received.

- There were 389,004 referrals active at any point during March for people aged under 19, of which 56,127 were new referrals and 41,559 people under 19 were discharged during the month.

- Of the 1,191,779 in contact with mental health services at the end of March, 284,599 (23.9 per cent) were aged under 19.

https://digital.nhs.uk/dataandinformation/publications/statisti cal/mental-health-servicesmonthly-statistics/mental-health-services-monthly-statisticsfinal-march-2018

ABORTIONS

Key points in 2017

- Total abortions have increased for residents of England & Wales 16.5 per 1,000 resident women had an abortion 2

- Abortions for non- residents of England & Wales decreased to the lowest level since 1968

- Over the last 10 years abortion rates have been decreasing for women aged under 25, particularly for women aged under 20.

- Abortion rates have been increasing for women aged 30 and over

- Almost all abortions in England & Wales were funded by the NHS in 2016, with most of these abortions taking place in the independent sector

- 9 out of 10 abortions were carried out under 13 weeks.

- 3,158 abortions were due to the risk that the child would be born seriously handicapped

- 65% of abortions were medically induced

- 39% of women who had an abortion had one or more previous abortions

- There were 189,8591 abortions for women resident in England and Wales in 2017 and 194,6681 abortions including nonresidents.

This is an increase of 2.3% since 2016, and a similar level to 2011.

- Abortion rate increased from 16.0 per 1,000 women in 2016. The rate has declined since 2007, when 17.9 per 1,000 of resident women had an abortion.

- 4,809 abortions for non-residents were carried out in England and Wales, a similar level to 2016. The 2017 total is a decrease of 35% since 2007.

- 64% of non-residents travel from the Republic of Ireland and 19% from Northern Ireland.

- The highest abortion rate is amongst women aged 20-24 (27.8 per 1,000 resident women). This is an increase on 2016 (27.0 per 1,000), but the rate has declined steadily since 2007 (32.6 per 1,000).

- The under 18 abortion rates for 2017 is 8.2 per 1,000 residents women. This is less than half the 2007 rate of 19.8 per 1,000.

- The abortion rate for 30-34-year old's was 18.2 per 1,000 residents women in 2016. This has increased from a rate of 15.1 per 1,000 women in 2007.

- 98% of abortions were funded by the NHS, the same level since 2013, but an increase from 88% in 2007.

- 70% of NHS funded abortions took place in the independent sector, an increase of 2 percentage points from 2016 and an increase from 50% in 2007.

- This figure has remained constant since 2007. Around four out of every five abortions were carried out under 10 weeks' gestation.

- This number of abortions represents 2% of the total number. This is a similar level to 2016 when there were 3,208 (2%) abortions for this reason.

- This is higher than in 2016 (62%), and almost double the proportion in 2007 (34%).

- This is slightly higher than 2016 (38%), but an increase of 7 percentage points since 2007.

https://assets.publishing.service.gov.uk/government/uploads/system/uploads/attachment_data/file/714183/2017_Abortion_Statistics_Commentary.pdf

SUICIDE

Here is a summary of the key trends contained in this report.

- In 2017 there were 6,213 suicides in the UK and Republic of Ireland.

- 5,821 suicides were registered in the UK and 392 occurred in the Republic of Ireland.

- In the UK men remain three times as likely to take their own lives than women, and in the Republic of Ireland four times more likely.

- The highest suicide rate in the UK was for men aged 45-49.

- The highest suicide rate in the Republic of Ireland was for men aged 25–34 (with an almost identical rate for men aged 45–54).

- There has been a significant decrease in male suicide in the UK, and the male suicide rate is the lowest in over 30 years.

- The suicide rate in Scotland decreased between 2016 and 2017 – this appears to be driven by a decrease in the female suicide rate.

- Suicide in young men in Scotland increased for the third consecutive year in 2017.

- Suicide has also continued to fall in both males and females in the Republic of Ireland.

Rates in the Republic of Ireland have fluctuated more than in the UK in recent years, but it is currently at its lowest since 1989.

https://www.samaritans.org/about-us/our-research/facts-andfigures-about-suicide

TEENAGE PREGNANCIES

Teenage pregnancy is a cause and consequence of education and health inequality for young parents and their children. Despite significant progress over the last 18 years, with a reduction of almost 60% in the under-18 conception rate, a continued focus is needed.

Teenagers have the highest rate of unplanned pregnancy with disproportionately poor outcomes (1).

Over 50% of under-18 conceptions end in abortion and inequalities remain between and within local authorities (2).

In 2016 babies born to mothers in England and Wales under 20 years had a 24% higher rate of stillbirth than average, and a 56% higher rate of infant mortality than average (3). Rates of low birthweight in younger mothers were 30% higher than average, and this inequality is increasing (4).

Children born to teenage mothers have a 63% higher risk of living in poverty (5). Mothers under 20 have a 30% higher risk of poor mental health two years after giving birth (6). This affects their own wellbeing, and their ability to form a secure attachment with their baby, recognised as a key foundation stone for positive child

outcomes (7). Teenage mothers are more likely than other young people to not be in education, employment or training (8); and by the age of 30, are 22% more likely to be living in poverty than mothers giving birth aged 24 or over (9). Young fathers are twice as likely to be unemployed aged 30, even after taking account of deprivation (10). Recent analysis of the Next Steps1 data shows that some of these poor outcomes are also experienced by young parents up to the age of 25 (11).

Since the introduction of the Teenage Pregnancy Strategy in 1999, England has achieved a 59.7% reduction in the under-18 conception rate between 1998 and 2016. The rate of 18.8 / 1000 is currently at the lowest level since 1969 (12), with the greatest reductions in the most deprived areas, and a doubling in the proportion of young mothers in education, training or employment (13). The success of the strategy's approach has been recognised by the World Health Organisation with the lessons being shared internationally with countries seeking to address high rates (14,15).

However, despite the significant progress England's teenage birth rate remains higher than comparable western European countries (16), and inequalities in the under-18 conception rate persist between and within local areas. Over a quarter of local authorities have an under-18 conception rate significantly higher than the England average (17) and 60% have at least one high rate ward (18).

Further progress in both reducing the under-18 conception rate and improving the outcomes for young parents is central to improving young people's sexual health and narrowing the health and educational inequalities experienced by young parents and their children. Maintaining the downward trend is a priority in the Department of Health Framework for Sexual Health Improvement in England (19) and key to PHE priorities, including reducing health inequalities, ensuring every child gets the best start in life and improving sexual and reproductive health (20). The Public Health Outcomes Framework (PHOF) includes the under-18 conception rate and a number of other indicators disproportionately affecting young parents and their children (21). The data shown below at local authority level shows the 2016 rates. The most recent conception rates for local authorities are available from Office for National Statistics.

Background, demographics and teenage pregnancy in Birmingham

As of 2016, Birmingham had a population of 21,238 girls aged 15 - 17 years.

There is a strong relationship between teenage conceptions and deprivation (22). Birmingham, with a score of 37.8, is in the most deprived decile (IMD 2015).

In Birmingham in 2016, 455 young women aged under 18 years conceived, which is a rate of 21.4 per 1,000 population. The national average was 18.8. In 2016 63 girls became pregnant under 16 years, a rate of 3.0 per 1,000 population; the national rate was 3.0. Of under 18 conceptions in Birmingham in 2016, 46.4% led to abortion, compared with the national average of 51.8%.

The charts and tables below show trends in under 18 and under 16 conceptions and abortions. The abortion rate (i.e. number of abortions per 1,000 population) is also displayed in the chart showing under-18 conceptions. The tables below the chart show the data for the conception rate, abortion rate and the percentage of conceptions leading to abortion.

https://fingertips.phe.org.uk/reports/ssrs/?reportName=chimat%2F
Teenage_pregnancy_young_parents&areaCode=E08000025&areaType
Id=102&parentCode=E12000005&parentTypeId=6&groupId=19381
32988&format=d

ACKNOWLEDGMENTS

I want to give thanks to God first and foremost as I wouldn't be here if it wasn't for him.

My Mum who has been my rock, supported me from day one, believed and encouraged me.

My Dad from whom I have inherited some of my creative skills, encouraged me in my dreams and always been proud.

Elijah and Jehlani my two sons and my nephew Kaleb who are my motivation and heartbeat.

My siblings Jonathan, Leah and Joshua, I have got nothing but love for.

Grandad and Grandma Simmonds, Grandma Brown for sharing with me their knowledge and love. I couldn't ask for better grandparents who have been my guide and role models they are what hard work looks like.

Auntie Tina who has always there when I need her even when I don't ask and supported me and my dreams always.

Auntie Rachel for writing my foreword, editing and being there to listen and run to as a child.

Auntie Aquila for partial editing and being a great eldest auntie.

Thanks to all Aunties, Uncles, Cousins of family, Bell, Brown, Griffin, Simmonds, Warner to say the least.

ends and family in alphabetical order Daryl Blenham, Candace Brown, Nicola Brown, Loretta Bryan, Deanne Bryan, Bryan family, Ricky Dawson, Teon Dunkley, Michael Ellis, Jenna Evans, Davinia Gayle, Ashley Hesson, Sabina Hunter, Aruja Jeraroopan, Niruja Jeraroopan, Ranjit Kaur, Rebecca Lee, Dominique Lewis, Abigail Mcbean, Lareasa Mulcare, Oliver Petrie, Jessica Petrie, Kady Power, Lushea Taylor, Nesia-Marie, Warner-Thomas, Chai lee Wong, Kyomi Wong who have all impacted in my life in some way. All are not named but I acknowledge you.

Past friends who were part of my growth and supported me at a time I acknowledge you.

Past partners who gave me the ignition to write A Womans Worth? so other young women growing up can know what not to go for and for giving me experiences that enabled me to grow, thank you too.

ABOUT THE AUTHOR

Born in Brum, multitalented Mother of two Chloe Rebekah is creative and passionate. She is inspired by the need for change, excited by new challenges and afraid of not maximising her potential. She says she'd love a life filled of smiling faces and laughter. Her naturally contagious personality is not one to be status quo, as in her words allows her to sustain her uniqueness as a person. If you could sum up Chloe in one word it'd be marmite there is no in-between.